KU-178-117

Granny Squares & Shapes

20 crochet projects
for you and your home

SUSAN PINNER

First published 2015 by
Guild of Master Craftsman Publications Ltd
Castle Place, 166 High Street, Lewes,
East Sussex BN7 1XU

Reprinted 2015

Text © Susan Pinner, 2015
Copyright in the Work © GMC Publications Ltd, 2015

ISBN 978-1-86108-752-2

All rights reserved

The right of Susan Pinner to be identified as the author
of this work has been asserted in accordance with
the Copyright, Designs and Patents Act 1988, sections
77 and 78.

No part of this publication may be reproduced, stored
in a retrieval system or transmitted in any form or by any
means without the prior permission of the publisher and
copyright owner.

This book is sold subject to the condition that all
designs are copyright and are not for commercial
reproduction without the permission of the designer
and copyright owner.

Whilst every effort has been made to obtain permission
from the copyright holders for all material used in this
book, the publishers will be pleased to hear from anyone
who has not been appropriately acknowledged and to
make the correction in future reprints.

The publishers and author can accept no legal
responsibility for any consequences arising from the
application of information, advice or instructions given
in this publication.

A catalogue record for this book is available from the
British Library.

Publisher: Jonathan Bailey
Production Manager: Jim Bulley
Senior Project Editor: Wendy McAngus
Editor: Cath Senker
Pattern Checker: Carol Ibbetson
Managing Art Editor: Gilda Pacitti
Art Editor: Luana Gobbo
Photographers: Christina Wilson and Andrew Perris

Set in Gibson
Colour origination by GMC Reprographics
Printed and bound in China

Contents

THE PROJECTS

Cotton Summer Slippers	56
Decorative Stool Cover	60
Flowery Hairband	64
Pillow Cover	68
Flower-petal Wrap	72
Vintage-look Beret	76
Beanie Bowl	80
Cami Top	84
Shawl Pin	88
Daisy Top	92
Bright Collar	96
Mini Bag	100
Foot Decoration	104
Heart Bunting	108
Colourful Dish	112
Triangle Lap Blanket	116
Pinwheel Shawl	120
Black-edged Lace Mat	124
Daisy Rug	128
Giant Cushion	132

Abbreviations	137
Conversions	137
Suppliers	138
Resources	140
Acknowledgements	142
Index	143

Introduction	8
Gallery of projects	10

GETTING STARTED

Tools	32
Yarns	34
Basic crochet techniques	36
Basic granny shapes	50
Colour, yarn and motif	53

Introduction

I'm so excited that my second book is now available and I do hope you love it as much as my first crochet book, *Granny Squares: 20 Crochet Projects with a Vintage Vibe*. It has 20 more adaptable designs for everyone from beginner to enthusiast to enjoy.

In this book I'm looking forward to sharing the next stage of my crochet journey – new ideas and lots more projects full of colour, interesting shapes and textures. I hope this journey will encourage and inspire even more people to take up the hook and to go forth with passion, colour and fabulously woolly thoughts.

Please experiment as some of you did with my first book. I love to see my ideas popping up on the internet with your very own slant on them; your wonderful colour combinations and choice of yarns is fabulous to see.

It seems strange now to remember that years ago I thought, "What could I possibly want with a computer?" I resisted technology, but how wrong I was because I wouldn't be writing this now if it wasn't for that technology.

The world now has a huge family of crochet addicts who can be found online, ready to share and help with ideas. All the crochet groups, across every country, all the local Knit and Natter groups that have sprung up everywhere are joining us all together across the world to be creative in a game of hooky. It's a truly international phenomenon.

Who would have predicted that old and young would come together to keep this fabulously colourful craft alive?

We have united in so many ways to create an exciting new crochet world, full of interesting patterns and motifs.

I think the humble beginnings of the granny square are something of a distant memory now. Almost every country has a crochet designer or two of worth, blogging, writing books and sharing their ideas and knowledge with this wonderful global crochet family.

This phenomenal crochet community is growing by the day, becoming a fantastic party full of friends from all around the world. So find that hook, sort out that stash and let's make this party rock!

Join the fun and let's play hooky!

Sue

COTTON SUMMER SLIPPERS
page 56

DECORATIVE
STOOL COVER
page 60

FLOWERY HAIRBAND
page 64

PILLOW COVER
page 68

FLOWER-PETAL WRAP
page 72

VINTAGE-LOOK BERET
page 76

BEANIE BOWL
page 80

CAMI TOP
page 84

SHAWL PIN
page 88

DAISY TOP
page 92

BRIGHT COLLAR
page 96

MINI BAG (AND PURSE)
page 100

FOOT DECORATION
page 104

HEART BUNTING
page 108

COLOURFUL DISH
page 112

TRIANGLE LAP BLANKET
page 116

PINWHEEL SHAWL
page 120

BLACK-EDGED LACE MAT
page 124

DAISY RUG
page 128

GIANT CUSHION
page 132

getting started

Tools

To get started all you really need is a hook, some yarn and a pair of scissors. Here are details of the basics and a number of other items that you may find useful as you crochet.

Crochet hooks

Hooks are made in a variety of materials including acrylic, steel, bamboo, wood, bone, plastic, aluminium and silver. Antique silver hooks are rare treasures, so look after them if you have them.

My favourites for a beginner to use are aluminium hooks. These affordable hooks have a flat middle where your thumb goes to stop the hook from spinning around while you work. Your yarns will slide easily over the hook. I'd also recommend trying hooks with Soft Touch handles. These days I wouldn't use anything else.

A good hook size to start with is 4mm (UK8:USG/6), used for most double-knit (DK) yarns. The recommended hook size will be stated on the ball bands of most yarns. If you are a keen crocheter, it may be worth buying a complete set of hooks, as they include a useful range of sizes.

Granny's tip

A good tip is to hang your scissors around your neck on a chain or ribbon. I was always looking for my scissors until I hung them around my neck!

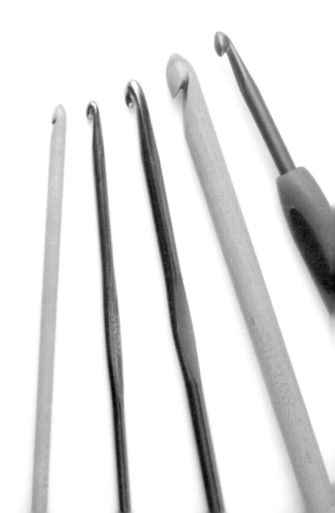

Scissors

A pair of small, round-ended scissors is essential for all crochet projects.

Yarn needle or bodkin

I always weave in the ends with the hook I am using, dealing with them as they happen. If you prefer, you can sew in the ends at the completion of a project using a yarn needle or bodkin.

Tape measure or ruler

You will need one of these to check that the tension, or square size, is correct and to work out how many squares you need for a project.

Granny's tip

Where the pattern states that a particular tension is required, always crochet a sample to check you are working to the correct tension.

Storage

Recycled tins with cute crochet covers are perfect for storing your hooks, scissors and needles. They can also be used as great storage containers for pens and pencils in your project kit.

For yarn storage, you can start with any bag or box, but as your stash grows you will need more and more room. If you are lucky enough to have the space, a designated cupboard is ideal. Plastic trugs are a cheap and cheerful storage idea – perfect if you take your work into the garden. Large, stackable plastic storage boxes are another great solution. You can be very creative with ways to store your yarns, so feel free to use your imagination!

Notebook and pen

I keep extensive notes and file all my ball bands with a small sample of the yarn. It might seem a bit of a hassle to do this but in the long run you will find it extremely useful. Making a note of the yarns, hook size and patterns you use means that you can easily check the details later on when you run out of yarn and need to re-stock. I guarantee that you will never remember what it is called or where you bought it, so keep a note.

Yarns

There is a whole world of yarns out there waiting to be enjoyed. You'll find some are easier to crochet with than others, while some come in more exciting colours or feel softer to the touch. The choice is yours!

Yarn weights

Yarns are sold in weights varying from light and lacy to super bulky. But be aware that even if two yarns are labelled as the same weight they can vary, even in the same brand.

All yarn weights have a place in the world of today's imaginative crocheter, so be adventurous and experiment with interesting yarns.

Choosing yarns for granny squares

Granny motifs can be made in most yarn types. Changing the hook size to suit the yarn can produce some exciting results – from delicate cotton lacy mats to chunky rugs. Never be afraid to experiment with yarn, colour and pattern. When you become more experienced, go for as many exquisite and exciting yarns as you can afford.

Acrylic Most beginners start off with acrylic because it is widely available, comes in a good range of colours and is affordable. Ribbon yarns can also be a good first choice if you want a yarn that won't split and is reasonably priced.

Wool and acrylic mix If your budget allows, buy a mix of wool and acrylic, usually with up to 70% wool. You will find a good choice of colours and it is acceptable to mix up brands as long as they are of similar weight. Superwash wool is another good choice – it will wash and wear well.

Pure merino wool This is another favourite of mine, particularly the oiled variety. It is slightly finer than the usual DK, but blooms after washing. It can be doubled up for a thick yarn and has a cotton-like appearance. It is easy to work with and can be found in a great range of colours.

Cotton If you have an allergy to wool, cotton is a good choice. Choose a brand with a firm twist, since the hook can sometimes split the yarn, causing much frustration. A cotton and bamboo mix or pure bamboo ribbon is another lovely yarn: beautifully soft and easy to work with.

Alpaca This is one of the nicest yarns and is often mixed with merino for a wonderful crochet experience.

Mohair and cashmere These are both wonderfully luxurious yarns, but they are expensive.

Doubling or mixing yarns

Mix two or more of the same or different yarns together and create your own unique blend. This will give a depth to any piece of work, adding great texture – just treat two strands as one.

Tension

A beginner often has difficulty with getting the correct tension. Don't grip the yarn so tightly that your hand and fingers ache. However, not gripping it tightly enough will result in loose and uneven stitches. Practice is the best solution; you could also try watching a friend crochet.

Base-chain runs often work up slightly tighter than the body of the work; try starting with a hook one size larger for the base chain, particularly on a long run of chain stitches, then continue with the correct size. Changing the hook size up or down a size can help to correct your tension when a specific size square is required.

Basic crochet techniques

To start you off, here are the basic techniques. In this book we use UK crochet terms. US terms are different, so always check which are used in a pattern before you start.

Granny's tip

When you work stitches back and forth on both sides, you create a double-sided piece of fabric. When you work in the round, your piece will have a front and a back. However, both sides look lovely and many people can't tell the difference!

Front

Back

Holding the hook and yarn

There are different ways to hold a crochet hook and you will find the one that suits you best as you progress. Here's how I work. Swap the hands if you are left-handed.

1 Hold the hook like a pen, with thumb and index finger on the flat bit of the hook for greatest control, in your right hand.

2 Wrap the yarn around the little finger of your left hand and grip it between the little finger and the ring finger to keep a good tension. The yarn then comes over the back of the hand with the middle finger stretched out a little to enable access to the yarn, and the crochet work is held by the index finger and thumb very close to the working stitch. You will need to move your grip closer every few stitches.

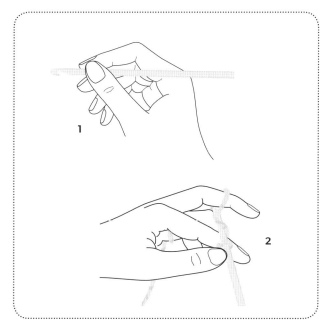

Slip knot (sl k)

The very first thing you will need to start your crochet is a slip knot. Hold the end of the yarn in your left hand, between your thumb and index finger, with about an inch (2.5cm) down your palm and the length of yarn over the back of your fingers. Bring the length around your fingers to make a full circle, then pull the length through the circle to make a loop. Holding the loop, pull the short end to form a loose knot, put your hook in the large loop and pull to tighten.

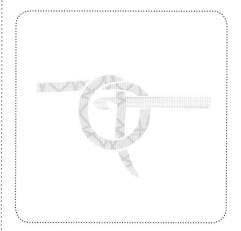

Chain stitch (ch)

This is the most basic of all crochet stitches, so the first you will learn as a beginner. It is also a very useful and creative stitch.

Chain stitches are used to begin most crochet projects and can be referred to as a starting chain, base chain or a foundation chain. A turning chain is often used between rows, and two or three chain stitches are used as a replacement for the first stitch to give the required height.

Chain stitches can be used to create some interesting effects, ranging from decorative loop combinations for edgings (picots) to button loops.

1 Start with a loop on your hook, then bring the yarn around the hook.

2 Pull the yarn through the first loop to form a chain stitch.

3 Repeat through each loop until you have the required number of chain stitches. Front view of chain is shown.

4 Back view of finished chain.

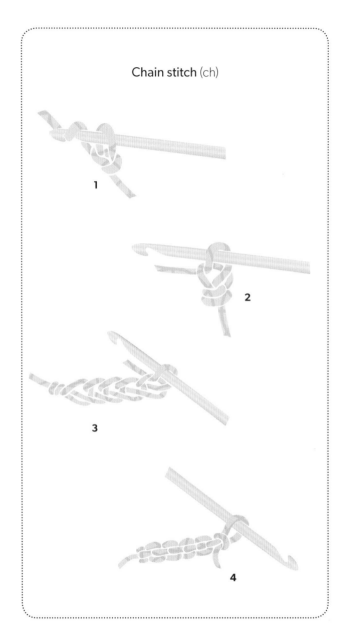

Chain stitch (ch)

Slip stitch (sl st)

More than just a joining stitch, slip stitch can be used as a decorative stitch or to create a crocheted fabric.

1 With a loop on your hook, push the hook through the base stitch, yarn over hook, pull through the stitch and the loop on the hook.

2 Repeat until you have the required number of stitches.

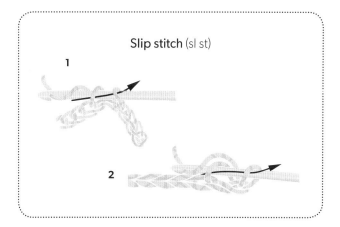

Slip stitch (sl st)

Double crochet (dc)

A short, firm stitch and one of the easiest stitches to master, double crochet can be made to look quite different depending on which loop you work it through.

1 With a loop on the hook, insert the hook through a base stitch, yarn over hook, pull through the base stitch only. You now have two loops on the hook.

2 Yarn over hook, pull through both loops. You now have a single loop on your hook and the double crochet stitch is complete.

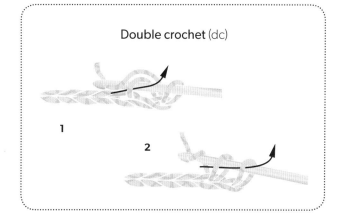

Double crochet (dc)

Double crochet long stitch (dc long stitch)

Also called spike stitch, this is a long decorative stitch made into one or more rows below the one you are working on. So instead of working into the two loops of the next stitch, work into the corresponding stitch in the row below the next stitch. Don't worry if it isn't directly below; a little to one side is normal. Work a spike stitch into lower rows if you like to make a longer spike.

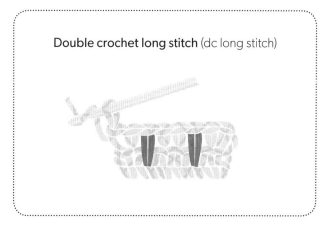

Double crochet long stitch (dc long stitch)

Treble crochet (tr)

The treble crochet is taller than the double crochet and probably the most used of the basic crochet stitches.

1 With a loop on your hook, yarn over hook (two loops), push hook through a base stitch.

2 Yarn over hook then pull through the base stitch. You now have three loops on your hook. Yarn over hook then pull through two of the loops. You now have two loops on your hook.

3 Yarn over hook then pull through last two loops.

4 You now have a single loop on the hook and the treble crochet stitch is complete.

Double treble (dtr)

This is similar to the treble, incorporating an extra step. Another well-used stitch, it is used to form corners and clusters in this book.

1 With a loop on your hook, wrap the yarn twice around the hook (three loops on the hook). Push the hook through a base stitch.

2 Yarn over hook and pull through (four loops on the hook).

3 Yarn over hook and pull through two of the loops. You now have three loops on the hook.

4 Yarn over hook and pull through two of the loops. You now have two loops on the hook.

5 Yarn over hook and pull through the last two loops. You now have a single loop on the hook and the double treble stitch is complete.

Double treble post stitch (dtr post stitch)

Yarn over hook. Insert the hook around the post of the stitch on the row below the one you are working on. Complete the stitch as usual, making sure you do not pull too tight.

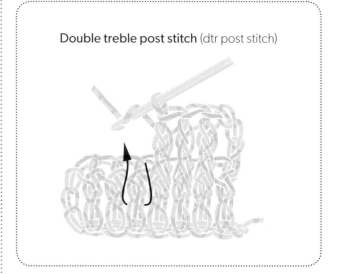

Double treble post stitch (dtr post stitch)

Treble crochet (tr)

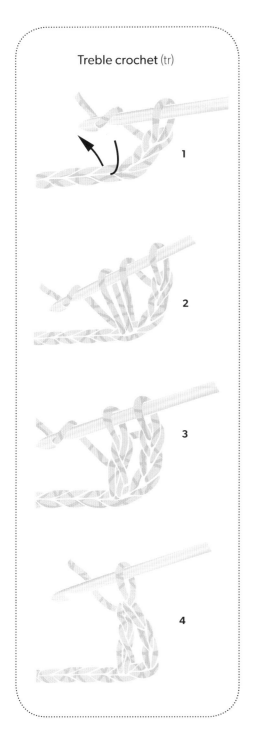

Double treble (dtr)

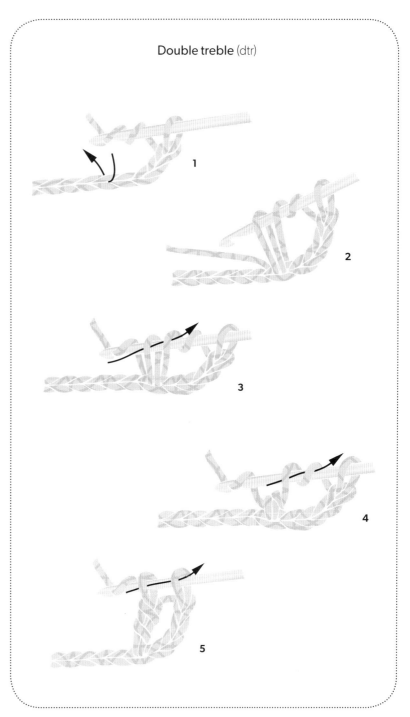

Cluster stitch

This is a half-made group of three or more treble or double treble stitches, worked into a single base stitch. They are drawn together on the last pull through. It is a great stitch for forming petal shapes and textured stitches.

Treble cluster

1 With a loop on the hook, yarn over hook and push through a base stitch. Yarn over hook and pull through (you'll have three loops on hook). Yarn over hook and pull through two loops. Hold the two loops on the hook. Repeat the beginning of the treble stitch two or three more times as required, into the same base stitch. (Clusters can be made of three, four or five stitches). Hold the last loop of each stitch on the hook until the group of half-made treble stitches is complete.

2 Yarn over the hook and pull through all the remaining loops, drawing all of the stitches together to make a cluster. Chain one to complete the stitch.

Double treble cluster

1 With a loop on the hook, yarn over hook twice (three loops on hook). Push hook through a base stitch, wrap yarn over hook and pull through (four loops on hook). Yarn over hook and pull through two loops (three loops on hook). Yarn over hook, pull through two loops (two loops remaining).

2 Repeat the beginning of the double treble stitch into the same base stitch, holding the last loop of each stitch on the hook, as many times as required.

3 Yarn over hook and pull through all of the remaining loops on the hook to draw all the stitches together to make a cluster. Complete the stitch with a chain stitch.

Shell stitch

A shell is a group of three or more completed treble stitches worked into one base stitch. Shells can be used in an all-over pattern, solid or open. Three trebles worked into the same space or stitch form the granny shell. Shells can be made with almost all crochet stitches in groups of three or more stitches. Shell stitch can be used to increase and also as a decorative edging stitch.

Increasing

Increases are made by doing two stitches into a single stitch of the round below and at regular intervals.

Decreasing

Decrease by missing a stitch or working two stitches together (dc2tog or tr2tog).
1 and 2 Do half of a stitch into each of the next two stitches, holding the loops on the hook.
3 Yarn over and pull through both stitches.

Granny's tip

For triple treble clusters, as used in the Shawl Pin on page 88, the method is the same as double treble cluster, except you need to wrap the yarn over the hook three times to start.

Basic crochet techniques

Treble cluster

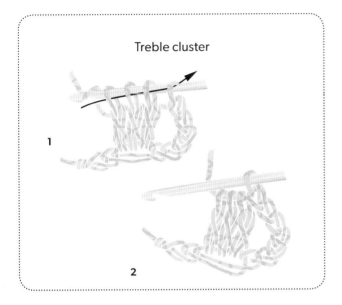

1

2

Shell stitch

Increasing

Double treble cluster

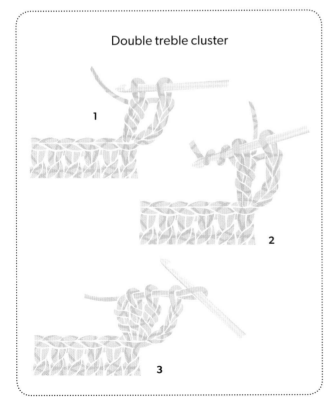

1

2

3

Decreasing

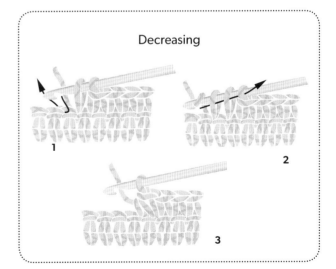

1

2

3

Working in the round

Working in the round is the basis for all granny motifs. First, you create a central base ring to work the first round into (using the chain circle, magic circle or finger-wrap techniques shown here). These can be different sizes depending on the design and whether or not a centre hole is required. Normally the hole will be filled with the first round of stitches that you crochet.

Depending on the stitch to be used in each round, a number of chain stitches are needed to get to the correct height for the stitch. You need one chain for a dc, two for a tr, three for a dtr and so on – each chain equal to each pull through of yarn. Each round is completed with a sl st into the top of the first st in the round.

Sometimes you work each round into the stitch and other times into the space between the stitches. This can make a big difference to the look of the design. If you are working in one colour and need to move from the end of one round to the next space, use a sl st into the top of the next few stitches to move across the top of the round to reach the next space, usually only a couple of stitches.

Because the first stitch is usually a set of chain stitches (to achieve the height), the beginning of a round sometimes shows up differently when the project is finished. To help disguise this, start each round at a different point rather than always in the same place. Staggering increase stitches in circular work will also help to hide the beginning and end of a round and keep a perfect circle. If you work increase stitches one on top of the other, a circle will turn into a hexagon quite quickly.

Chain circle

I usually use a four-chain circle that will take 12 or 16 stitches easily. Sometimes the chain circle becomes part of the design and a much larger number of chain stitches is used, forming a hole at the centre of the motif. Make a chain circle as stated in the pattern and join it to make a ring by making a slip stitch into the first chain.

Magic circle

Make a magic circle to give a very tight centre.
1   Make a half-formed slip knot.
2   Do all the first-round stitches into the circle.
3   Pull the end tight after completing one round.

Finger wraps

1   Wrap the yarn around one or two fingers the number of times stated in the pattern. A finger wrap of three wraps is shown here.

2   Slide the loops off your finger, holding them tightly, and insert the hook.

3   Make the stitches as instructed into all of the rings until the round is complete.

4   There are no knots, and you cannot see where the stitches begin or end.

Weaving in ends

I advise you to weave your ends into the back of the stitch at the start and finish of a round and crochet over them. If you leave them until a project is finished there can be a huge number to deal with. On a large, multicoloured bed blanket there could be literally thousands of ends. I always weave in the ends with the hook I am using, never leaving a square until all the ends have been hidden.

Basic crochet techniques

Chain circle

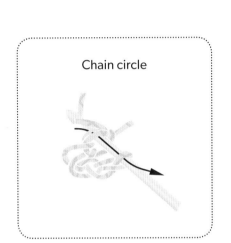

Magic circle

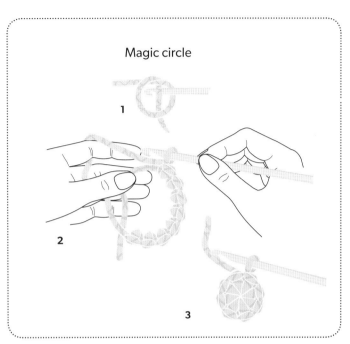

Finger wraps

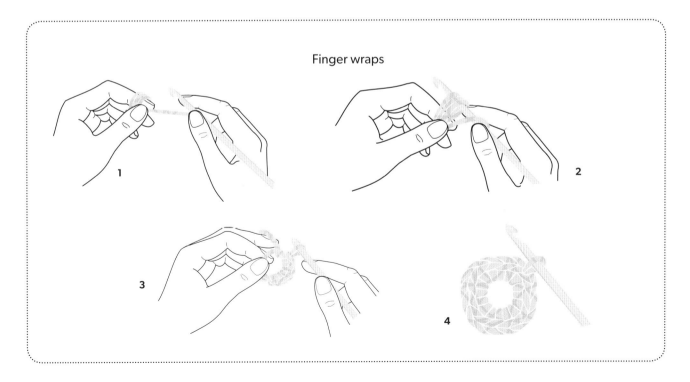

Joining your squares together

There are several techniques used for joining your squares together. Always use the same yarn as the project and use a large bodkin or a hook of the same size used in the project. I prefer to crochet squares together whenever possible but sometimes sewing your squares together is a good option. If the squares have the same last-round colour, you match the corresponding stitches and stitch them using one of the methods described. If your squares are all different colours, crocheting them together is a far better method.

Join as you go

This is a simple method of passing the hook through the matching space or stitch of a second square while crocheting the last round. Sometimes you can 'join as you go' using every stitch instead of using just the matched spaces to join squares/hexagons together. You can use this method for joining circles, but great care and only a few joining stitches are needed to prevent distortion of the circle.

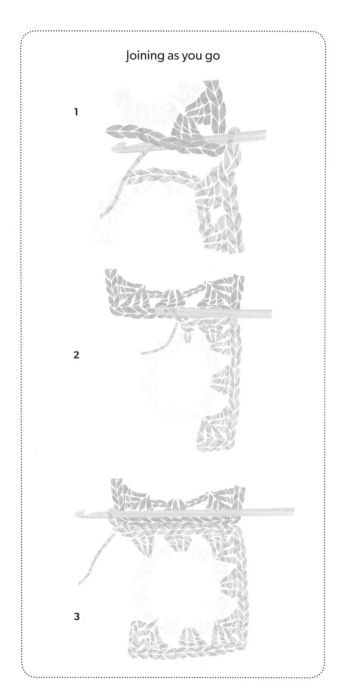

Joining as you go

1 — 2 — 3

1 Complete the first square. Work a second square up to the last round. You will use the final row to join the two squares. Join the yarn in the corner of the second square. Work the starting chain stitches and two tr sts. Ch 1, sl st to the corresponding chain-one space in the corner of the first square, ch 1. Return to the second square. 3 tr sts to complete corner.

2 Sl st into the corresponding space in the first square, pull yarn through hook. 3 tr sts in second square.

3 Repeat step 2 to the end of the row. In the corner, 3 tr sts, ch 1, sl st into corner of first square, ch 1, 3 tr sts. Complete the round on the second square.

Sewing up

Over stitch or whip stitch

Put two squares together one on top of the other, with right sides facing. Then over stitch, as shown, through the back loops only. This will give a neat ridge on the right side of your project.

Double crochet seams

Place two squares wrong sides together and, matching stitch for stitch, make a dc stitch through both edges of the two squares. This will give a decorative line of stitches if a contrast yarn colour has been used.

Mattress stitch

Matching corresponding stitches are worked back and forth from one edge stitch to the other, pulling the yarn tight after doing three or four stitches. The stitches should disappear inside the work, almost like adding another stitch between the squares.

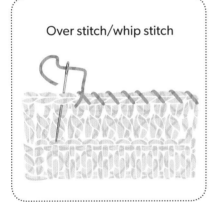

Over stitch/whip stitch

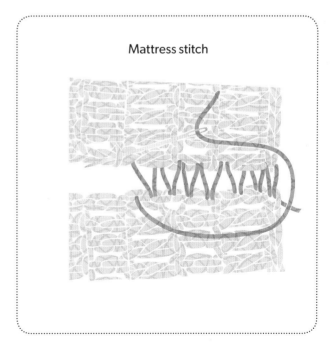

Mattress stitch

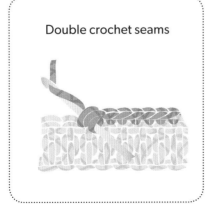

Double crochet seams

Care instructions

Washing instructions are usually found on yarn ball bands, so follow them. If you have mixed different yarns together you will need to take extra care. I always launder with a gentle wash on an 86°F (30°C) setting just in case I have used a pure wool that could felt or shrink. Spin and dry flat, gently pulling the work into shape. Very occasionally I use a tumble drier but *only* on a cool setting.

Granny's tip

Always keep your ball bands so you can refer to the washing instructions, hook size, name and content of the yarn, which could be useful at a later date or could be passed to the recipient of a crocheted gift.

Blocking your crochet

Blocking will give a finished and professional look to your work. It will shape and set a project, removing wobbles, waves and any distortions. You can dry block or wet block – always following the care instructions on ball bands.

Dry blocking: Lay your dry project out and pin (always use rust-proof pins) into shape on a wet towel, padded board or clean protected carpet and leave to dry.

Wet blocking: Lay your wet project out and pin (always use rust-proof pins) into shape. Spray or lightly steam and then leave to dry.

NEVER steam man-made yarns, such as acrylic, or hairy yarns, such as mohair or angora. If in doubt, do not block. Hours of work can be destroyed in seconds. I often wait until something needs washing before blocking it.

Problem solving

If your granny shapes look wobbly and uneven
You may have too many stitches for the circumference.

If your granny shapes are curling or cupping
You may not have enough stitches for the circumference.

If you miss a stitch or make a mistake
Unless it is an essential or very visible stitch, don't worry about it. No one will ever find it in a big project, but on a small project it is better to unpick and redo it.

If you run out of yarn a stitch or two from the end of a round
If you just run out by a couple of stitches you can undo a few stitches and then redo them, tightening the tension a little. By doing this, you can often gain enough yarn to do those last couple of stitches.

If you are not in the right place to start the next round
Use slip stitch to move across the top of a previous round to reach the starting space.

If you have problems keeping your yarn clean and tangle-free
Use zip-lock bags for each ball of yarn or use wet-wipe containers with a hole in the top – this will keep your yarn clean and stop it tangling.

If a square or hexagon looks uneven
Check the stitch count – each side of a square or hexagon should have the same number of stitches. Otherwise it may be that your tension is not even.

If your work feels too tight or stiff
A looser tension is needed, so go up a hook size. Do the opposite if the work feels loose and floppy. Find the right hook for the yarn to get the right feel for your work.

If your circles are frilly
Try the '12, 24, 36' rule. Start with a first round of 12 tr sts, second round is 24 tr sts, third round is 36 tr sts. An increase of 12 stitches in each round spread evenly should give you a flat circle in any yarn.

Basic granny shapes

Just because they are granny shapes, doesn't mean they have to be square! Practise these different variations for three or four rounds and then join them together to make whatever you like. Or you can just keep on going to create a giant shape.

Granny square

The granny square is worked from the centre on a base ring of chain stitches and made up of rounds of granny shells (usually three trebles) along each side with chain-stitch corners. These ones use four colours, A–D.

Four-round granny square

Using colour A, ch 4, sl st to form a ring, or use a magic circle or a finger wrap (see page 44).

Round 1: Using colour A, ch 2 (counts as 1 tr), 2 tr, ch 2, *3 tr, ch 2, repeat from * 2 more times, sl st to complete round (4 sides/4 corners).

Round 2: Using colour B, join to corner ch space, ch 2 (counts as 1 tr), (2 tr, ch 2, 3 tr) in same corner space, ch 1 *(3 tr, ch 2, 3 tr) in next corner space, ch 1, repeat from * 2 more times, sl st to complete round, weave in ends (2 groups of 3 tr, for each side).

Round 3: Using colour C, join to corner ch space, ch 2 (counts as 1 tr), (2 tr, ch 2, 3 tr) in corner space, ch 1, 3 tr in side space, ch 1 *(3 tr, ch 2, 3 tr) in corner space, ch 1, 3 tr, ch 1, repeat from * 2 more times, sl st to complete round, weave in ends (3 groups of 3 tr, for each side).

Round 4: Using colour D, join to corner ch space, ch 2 (counts as 1 tr), (2 tr, ch 2, 3 tr) in same corner space, ch 1, (3 tr, ch 1) in 2 side spaces, *(3 tr, ch 2, 3 tr) in corner space, ch 1, (3 tr, ch 1) in 2 side spaces, repeat from * 2 more times, sl st to complete round, weave in ends (4 groups of 3 tr, for each side).

Granny's tip

A one- or two-chain corner creates a rounded corner with a small hole. A three-chain corner gives a squarer, sharper corner with a bigger hole.

Granny circle

There are a number of variations on the granny circle motif. This particular combination will produce a flat granny circle.

Four-round granny circle

Using colour A, ch 4, sl st to form a ring.

Round 1: Using colour A, ch 3 (counts as 1 tr and ch space), *1 tr, ch 1, repeat from * 4 more times, sl st to complete round (6 spokes).

Round 2: Using colour B, ch 2 (counts as 1 tr), 1 tr, (ch 1, 2 tr, ch 1) in first space, *(2 tr, ch 1, 2 tr, ch 1) in next space, repeat from * in each space, sl st to complete round (12 groups of 2 tr plus ch).

Round 3: Using colour C, ch 2 (counts as 1 tr), 2 tr in first space, *3 tr in next space, repeat from * in each space, sl st to complete round (12 groups of 3 tr).

Round 4: Using colour D, ch 2 (counts as 1 tr), 2 tr, ch 1 in first space, *3 tr, ch 1 in next space, repeat from * in each space, sl st to complete round (12 groups of 3 tr plus ch).

Granny hexagon

These attractive six-sided shapes are easily joined into fabulous and decorative projects, each hexagon shape fitting exactly into the next in a staggered pattern.

Four-round granny hexagon

Using colour A, ch 6, sl st to form a ring.

Round 1: Using colour A, ch 2 (counts as 1 tr), 2 tr, ch 1, *3 tr, ch 1, repeat from * 4 more times, sl st to complete round (6 groups of 3 tr and ch 1).

Round 2: Using colour B, ch 2 (counts as 1 tr), (1 tr, ch 2, 2 tr) in same space, *(2 tr, ch 2, 2 tr) in next space, repeat from * in each space, sl st to complete round (12 groups of 2 tr).

Round 3: Using colour C, ch 2 (counts as 1 tr), (1 tr, ch 2, 2 tr) in corner space, 2 tr in side space, *(2 tr, ch 2, 2 tr) in corner space, 2 tr in side space, repeat from * 4 more times, sl st to complete round (18 groups of 2 tr).

Round 4: Using colour D, ch 2 (counts as 1 tr), 2 tr, 2 ch, 3 tr in corner space, 3 tr in side spaces, repeat 5 more times, sl st to complete round (24 groups of 2 tr).

Colour, yarn and motif

Once you've learned the basics the next stage is the marrying of yarn, motif and colours together. It isn't the easiest process, but it is certainly the most exciting.

Choosing colour combinations

Colour is a personal thing and it has different associations for different people. I still get it wrong sometimes, even after 40-plus years of study. My motto is, if in doubt use them all – a rainbow always looks good, doesn't it?

If you are struggling to get started, choose lots of shades of a favourite colour. Use some dark and some light to give depth, and then use every shade in between. Join your squares together with cream, white or black – each of these neutrals will pull everything together. Some very random granny squares can be made to look fabulous and quite on-trend when joined together with a neutral colour – something that makes all those beautiful colours zing.

Add a border using a combination of all the colours or black and white – these always make for an interesting frame to a blanket or throw. Use punched squares, circles and flowers to create a blanket on paper before you commit to expensive yarn buying.

Get inspired

Inspiration can come from many places – a colourful picture or flowery mug, your garden, the room you want to put your blanket or cushion in, a favourite colourful dress, wallpaper patterns and magazine images. Interiors and gardening magazines are good sources for colour inspiration. Study the great colourists of today; Kaffe Fassett and Tricia Guild are two of my favourites. Experiment with different colour combinations of yarns then make notes on anything you love.

the
projects

Cotton Summer Slippers

These lightweight cotton slippers made from diamond-shaped motifs are perfect for padding around at home or popping in your suitcase when you go on holiday. The slippers have a shaped heel for a great fit.

Finished size

To fit UK size 4–5/US size 6–7/EU size 37–38. Use a larger hook to make a bigger size.

You will need

• Approximately 3oz (80g) in total of cotton DK in 5 different colours (A–E in pattern). I used Stylecraft Classique Cotton DK in Azure (A), Poppy (B), Tropical Jade (C), Soft Lime (D) and Greek Blue (E).
• 4mm (UK8:USG/6) crochet hook

Tension

Front diamond motif and sole motifs measure 4½ x 5½in (11.5 x 14cm). Side motif measures 4¼ x 5½in (11 x 14cm). Heel motif measures 3 x 4½in (7.5 x 11.5cm). Use a larger or smaller hook if necessary to obtain correct tension.

Front diamond motif
(make 1 for each slipper)

Using A, make a 2-finger wrap of 4 wraps (see page 44) or ch 10, sl st to form a ring.

Round 1: Using A, ch 2 (counts as 1 tr), 23 tr into circle, sl st to complete round (24 sts).

Round 2: Using B, attach yarn in any st, ch 5 (counts as 1 tr and ch 3 sp), tr into same st, tr into next 5 sts, *(tr, ch 3, tr) in next st, tr in next 5 sts, repeat from * to end, sl st to complete round, cut and weave in end (7 tr for each side).

Round 3: Using C, attach yarn in any ch 3 sp, ch 4 (counts as a 1 dtr, and ch 1 sp), (dtr, ch 3, dtr, ch 1, dtr) into same sp, *(ch 1, miss 1 st, tr into next st) 3 times, ch 1, miss 1 st, (tr, ch 3, tr) into next ch sp, (ch 1, miss 1 st, tr into next st) 3 times, ch 1, miss 1 st, (dtr, ch 1, dtr, ch 3, dtr, ch 1, dtr) into ch sp, repeat from * to end, finishing with ch 1, miss 1 st, sl st to complete round, cut and weave in end (24 ch sps).

Round 4: Using D, attach yarn at the top of the diamond motif, ch 2 (counts as 1 tr), 2 tr, ch 2, 3 tr) into same sp, *2 tr into next 5 sp, (2 tr, ch 2, 2 tr) into next sp, 2 tr into next 5 sp, (3 tr, ch 2, 3 tr) into next sp, repeat from * to end, finishing with 2 tr, sl st to complete round, cut and weave in end.

Sole motif
(make 1 for each slipper)

Using E for the whole motif, magic circle or ch 4, sl st into a circle.

Round 1: Ch 2 (counts as 1 tr), 11 tr into circle, sl st to complete round (12 sts).

Round 2: Ch 2 (counts as 1 tr), 1 tr into same st, 2 tr in the next 11 sts, sl st to complete round (24 sts).

Round 3: Ch 3 (counts as 1 dtr), (dtr, ch 3, 2 dtr) into same st, *dtr into next st, tr into next 4 sts, (2 tr, ch 2, 2 tr) into next st, tr into next 4 sts, dtr into next st, (2 dtr, ch 3, 2 dtr) into next st, repeat from * to end, finishing with a tr, sl st to complete round (9 sts each side).

Round 4: Ch 2 (counts as 1 tr), *2 tr into next st, (3 dtr, ch 2, 3 dtr) into ch sp, 2 tr into next st, tr into next 8 sts, (2 tr, ch 2, 2 tr) into next ch sp, tr into next 8 sts, 2 tr into next st, (3 dtr, ch 2, 3 dtr) into next ch sp, 2 tr into next st, tr into next 8 sts, (2 tr, ch 2, 2 tr) into next ch sp, tr into next 7 sts, sl st to complete round, cut and weave in end (15 sts each side).

Side motif
(make 2 for each slipper)

Using A, make a 2-finger wrap of 4 wraps or ch 10, sl st to form a ring.

Round 1: Using A, ch 2 (counts as 1 tr), 23 tr into circle, sl st to complete round (24 sts).

Round 2: Using B, attach yarn in any st, ch 3 (counts as 1 dtr), (dtr, ch 3, 2 dtr) into first st, *dtr into next st, tr into next 4 sts, (2 tr, ch 2, 2 tr) into next st, tr into next 4 sts, dtr into next st, (2 dtr, ch 3, 2 dtr) into next st, repeat from * to end, finishing with a dtr, sl st to complete round (9 sts each side).

Round 3: Using D, attach yarn at the top of the diamond motif, ch 3 (counts as 1 dtr), (2 dtr, ch 2, 3 dtr) into ch sp, *2 tr into next st, tr into next 8 sts, (2 tr, ch 2, 2 tr) into next ch sp, tr into next 8 sts, 2 tr into next st, (3 dtr, ch 2, 3 dtr) into next ch sp, rep from * to end, finishing with 2 tr, sl st to complete round, cut and weave in end (15 sts each side).

Heel motif
(make 1 for each slipper)

Using A, make a finger wrap of 4 wraps or ch 6, sl st into a circle.

Round 1: Using A, ch 2 (counts as tr), 14 tr into circle, sl st to complete round, cut and weave in end (15 sts).

Round 2: Using B, attach yarn in any st, ch 2 (counts as tr), (tr, ch 2, 2 dtr) into same st, dtr into next 2 sts, (2 dtr, ch 2, 2 tr) into next st, tr into next 5 sts, (2 dtr, ch 3, 2 dtr) into next st, tr into next 5 sts, sl st to complete round, cut and weave in end (24 sts).

Round 3: Using D, attach yarn in first ch 2 sp, ch 2 (counts as tr), (tr, ch 2, dtr) in same ch sp, dtr in next 6 sts, (dtr, ch 2, 2 tr) in next ch sp, tr in next 8 sts, 2 tr in next st, (3 dtr, ch 3, 3 dtr) in next ch sp, 2 tr in next st, tr in next 8 sts, sl st to complete round, cut and weave in end (38 sts).

Making up

Use round 4 of front and sole motif and round 3 of sides and heel motifs to join together as you go (see page 46); alternatively, sew all the motifs together following chart sequence.

Finishing

Around the opening of the slipper, using D, start at the front of the slipper.

Round 1: Ch 1 (counts as dc), dc in next 13 sts, 2 tr into ch sp, tr into joining st, tr in next 6 sts, tr in joining st, 2 tr into ch sp, dc into next 14 sts, miss 1 st, sl st to complete round (40 sts).

Round 2: Ch 1 (counts as 1 dc), dc in next 14 sts, tr in next 12 sts, dc into next 14 sts, miss 1 st, sl st to complete round. Cut and weave in end (40 sts).

granny's tip

You can add waterproof PVA glue to the soles to make them non-slip.

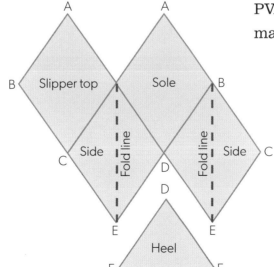

Decorative Stool Cover

This attractive cover for a stool of 12in (30cm) diameter uses less than 3oz (80g) of DK cotton. It is made in nine colours and finished with five rounds of granny shells. Co-ordinate it with your room colours or be creative with your leftover cottons.

Finished size

To fit a stool top 12in (30cm) in diameter. Add extra rounds for a bigger stool top or subtract rounds for a smaller one.

You will need

- Approximately 3oz (80g) of cotton DK in each of 9 colours (A, B, C, D, E, F, G, H and J in pattern).

  Multi colourway: I used purples, yellow and ochre, in Stylecraft Classique Cotton DK and King Cole Bamboo Cotton.

  Red and blue colourway: I used reds and blues, in Stylecraft Classique Cotton DK only.
- 4mm (UK8:USG/6) crochet hook

Tension

Not crucial to this project.

Stool cover

Using A, make a finger wrap of 4 wraps (see page 44) or ch 5, sl st to complete round.

Round 1: Using A, work 16 dc into the circle, sl st to complete round, cut and weave in ends (16 sts).

Round 2: Using B, attach yarn in any st, ch 2 (counts as tr), tr in next st, ch 4, *tr in next 4 sts, ch 4, repeat from * to end, finishing with tr in last 2 sts, sl st to complete round (4 loops).

Round 3: Continue using B, *4 tr, ch 3, 4 tr into loop, miss 2 sts, sl st into next sp, miss 2 sts, repeat from * to end, sl st to complete round, cut and weave in end (4 petals).

Round 4: Using C, attach yarn at point of petal, *ch 5, dtr into sl st of round 3 (dip of petal), ch 5, dc into point, repeat from * to end, sl st to complete round (8 ch loops).

Round 5: Continue using C (straight into the first ch loop), 9 dc into each ch loop, sl st to complete round, cut and weave in end (72 sts).

Round 6: Using D, attach yarn in the first dc of any loop, ch 1 (counts as dc), dc in next 2 sts, ch 6, *dc in next 3 sts, ch 6, repeat from * to end, sl st to complete round, cut and weave in end (24 loops).

Multi colourway

Round 7: Using C, attach yarn in any loop, ch 3, *dc in next loop, ch 3, repeat from * to end, sl st to complete round (24 loops).

Round 8: Continue using C, 4 dc into each ch 3 loop, sl st to complete round, cut and weave in end (96 sts).

Round 9: Using B, ch 2 (counts as tr), tr in every st, sl st to complete round, cut and weave in end (96 sts).

Round 10: Using E, attach yarn in any st, dc in every st, sl st to complete round, cut and weave in end (96 sts).

Round 11: Using F, attach yarn in any st, ch 2 (counts as tr), tr in next st, ch 2, miss 1 st, *tr in next 2 sts, ch 2, miss 1 st, repeat from * to end, sl st to complete round, cut and weave in end (32 holes).

Round 12: Using G, attach yarn in any first tr, dc in next st, 2 tr into the round 10 st under the missed st of round 11, *dc in next 2 sts, 2 tr into round 10 st under the missed st of round 11, repeat from * to end, sl st to complete round (128 sts).

Round 13: Continue using G, ch 2 (counts as tr), tr in every st, sl st to complete round, cut and weave in end (128 sts).

Round 14: Using H, ch 2 (counts as tr), tr in every st, sl st to complete round, cut and weave in end (128 sts).

Round 15: Using J, ch 2 (counts as tr), 2 tr in same st, miss 2 sts, *3 tr in next st, miss 2 sts, repeat from * to end, finishing with missing 1 st, sl st to complete round, cut and weave in end (43 granny shells).

Rounds 16–18: Using D, G, H in turn, attach yarn between any two granny shells from previous round, ch 2 (counts as tr), 2 tr in same space, miss granny shell, *3 tr in next space, miss granny shell, repeat from * to end, sl st to complete round, cut and weave in end (43 granny shells).

Rounds 19–20: Using H, ch 2 (counts as tr), tr in same sp, 2 tr in every sp, sl st to complete round, cut and weave in end (43 small granny shells).

Red and blue colourway

granny's tip

This pattern can also be used to make a placemat – just stop at any round after round 10 and before round 14.

Flowery Hairband

Pretty hair decorations are very popular, and this simple
hairband is an extremely quick project to make
from leftover cotton or mohair. You can also sew
single flowers individually to hairclips.

Finished size

11in (28cm), plus ties

You will need

- Small quantities of cotton or mohair yarns in lots of colours. Use two colours for each flower (A and B in pattern). I used Stylecraft Classique Cotton DK and Stylecraft Senses in various colours.
- 4mm (UK8:USG/6) crochet hook

Tension

Not crucial to this project.

Hairband

Using A, make a magic circle (see page 44) or ch 3, sl st into a circle.

Round 1: Using A, ch 2 (counts as tr), 2 tr into circle, ch 3, *3 tr, ch 3, repeat from * twice more, sl st to complete round, pull magic circle tight, cut and weave in ends (4 granny shells).

Round 2: Using B, attach yarn in any ch sp, *(ch 2, 2 tr, ch 2, sl st, ch 2, 2 tr, ch 2, sl st) into same sp, ch 1, sl st into next ch sp, repeat from * 3 times more, sl st to complete round.

Make four more flowers, join as you go (see page 46) or stitch 5 flowers tog in a row.

Ring-end ties
(make 2)

Using any colour, attach yarn into the sp between two petals of an end flower, ch 67, 12 dc in 2nd st from the hook to make a small ring, sl st to complete round, cut and weave in the ends.

granny's tip

Individual flowers made in white cotton and sewn onto clips would make great wedding hair decorations.

Pillow Cover

This decorative pillow cover can be made with
a large flower motif and two small ones on one side,
and six small motifs on the other side. Alternatively, you
can use six small motifs in different colours on each side.

Finished size

To fit a standard pillow 26 x 20in
(66 x 51cm)

You will need

- Approximately 15oz (425g) in total
  of Alpaca Merino Aran in 8 colours
  (A–H in pattern). I used Rooster
  Almerino Aran in Mushroom (A),
  Custard (B), Gooseberry (C),
  Brighton (D), Ocean (E), Hazelnut
  (F), Coral (G) and Beach (H).
- Stitch marker (optional)
- 4.5mm (UK7:US7) crochet hook
- 5 large buttons, approximately 1in
  (2.5cm) diameter

Tension

Not crucial to this project.

Large circle motif

Using A, make a 2-finger wrap of
4 wraps (see page 44) or ch 9, sl st
into a circle.

Round 1: Using A, 16 dc into the
circle, sl st to complete round, cut
and weave in end (16 sts).

Round 2: Using B, attached to
any st, ch 3 (counts as 1 dtr), 3 dtr
cluster (1 dtr in same st as starting
ch, 2 dtr in next st), ch 4, *4 dtr
cluster (2 dtr in each of next 2 sts),
ch 4, repeat from * to end, sl st to
complete round, cut and weave in
end (8 petals).

Round 3: Using C, attached to any
loop, ch 2 (counts as 1 tr), (2 tr, ch 1,
3 tr) in same loop, *(3 tr, ch 1, 3 tr) in
next loop, repeat from * to end, sl st
to complete round, cut and weave in
end (16 granny shells).

Round 4: Using D, attach yarn in the
first st in any loop, ch 2 (counts as
1 tr), tr in next 2 sts, ch 6, *tr in next
6 sts, ch 6, repeat from * to end,
finish with tr in last 3 sts, sl st into first
st (8 loops).

Round 5: Continue using D, work
11 tr into loop, miss 2 sts, dc into the
sp before next st, miss 2 sts, *11 tr
in next loop, miss 2 sts, dc into the
sp before next st, repeat from * to
end, sl st to complete round, cut and
weave in end (8 petals).

Round 6: Using E, attach yarn in 6th
st of any petal, *ch 6, miss 5 sts, dtr
into the next st (dip of petal), ch 6,
miss 5 sts, dc into next st, repeat
from * to end, sl st to complete
round (16 loops).

Round 7: Continue using E,
ch 2 (counts as 1 tr), 7 tr into first
loop, 8 tr into every loop, sl st to
complete round, cut and weave in
end (128 sts).

Round 8: Using A, dc in every st, sl
st to complete round, cut and weave
in end (128 sts).

Round 9: Using F, attach yarn to
st above the last st in a loop from
round 6, ch 2 (counts as tr), tr in next
st, ch 2, miss 2 sts, *tr in next 2 sts,
ch 2, miss 2 sts, repeat from * to
end, sl st to complete round, cut and
weave in end (32 holes).

Round 10: Using B, attach yarn
between any 2 tr, ch 2 (counts as tr),
2 tr in same st, miss the ch 2 sp, *3
tr between the next 2 tr, miss the ch
2 sp, repeat from * to end, sl st to
complete round, cut and weave in
end (32 granny shells).

Granny-shell corners

A granny-shell corner is half a 3-round granny square, with extra sts to accommodate the curve of the circle, and will turn your circles into easy-to-join squares. Mark four corners on each circle with a st marker or length of yarn (every 8 granny shells).

Round 1: Using A, attach yarn to 1 granny shell before marker, ch 1, miss 1 granny shell, (3 dtr, ch 4, 3 dtr) in next sp, (marked st), ch 1, miss 1 granny shell, sl st into next st, ch 3, miss 1 granny shell, sl st into next st, turn (2 granny shells).

Round 2: Continue using A, 2 dtr into the sp between circle and last dtr of round 1, ch 1, (3 dtr, ch 4, 3 dtr) into the next sp (point of triangle), ch 1, 3 dtr into next ch 1 sp (between the last granny shell and the circle), ch 1, miss 1 granny shell, sl st into next st, ch 3, miss 1 granny shell, sl st into next st, turn (4 granny shells).

Round 3: Continue using A, 2 dtr into first ch 1 sp, ch 1, 3 dtr into next ch 1 sp, ch 1, (3 dtr, ch 4, 3 dtr) in next ch sp (point of triangle), ch 1, 3 dtr into next ch 1 sp, ch 1, 3 dtr between circle and granny triangle, ch 1, miss 1 granny shell, sl st into next sp, cut off and weave in end (6 granny shells).

Granny-shell rounds

Use this colour order for the final granny-shell rounds:

Round 1: Using G, start in a corner, ch 2 (counts as tr), (2 tr, ch 2, 3 tr, ch 1) in same sp, *3 dc in next sp, ch 1, repeat from * to end of first side, (3 tr, ch 2, 3 tr) in corner sp, repeat side and corners to end of round, sl st to complete round, cut and weave in end (44 granny shells).

Round 2: Repeat granny-shell round in F (48 granny shells).

Round 3: Repeat granny-shell round in E (52 granny shells).

Round 4: Repeat granny-shell round in A (56 granny shells).

Round 5: Repeat granny-shell round in H (60 granny shells).

Round 6: Repeat granny-shell round in F (64 granny shells).

Round 7: Repeat granny-shell round in E (68 granny shells).

Round 8: Repeat granny-shell round in A (72 granny shells). Use this round to join as you go (see page 46). Join the large square to two small squares and the front to the back of the pillow. Alternatively, make a front and a back and join them together using dc, matching each st, and leaving an opening.

Small motif

Follow pattern for large motif to round 6.

Round 7: Continue using E, *7 dc into next loop, rep from * to end, sl st to complete round, cut and weave in end.

Granny-shell corner

To turn the circle into a square, add granny-shell corners as described for the large motif but do 2 rounds only. Use 4 of the dtr as the corner points.

Joining round

Make 7 granny shells for each side. In each corner sp, granny shell, ch 2, granny shell.

Finishing

Add 4 rows of dc to an opening that could be left at one end or along 2 small squares in the back. Sew on the buttons, spacing them evenly, and use the holes in the granny shells as buttonholes.

Flower-petal Wrap

This long wrap is made from 20 granny-square motifs, joined with chain loops to create a lacy pattern. You can add a drawstring to the wrap to create gathered ends, or leave the ends square and secure with a wrap pin.

Finished size

74 x 13½in (188 x 34cm)

You will need

- 1¾oz (50g) in each of 7 different colours (A–G in pattern) and 3½oz (100g) in background colour (H in pattern) of 100% merino yarn. I used James C Brett and Janet Watson 100% Merino DK in Beige (A), Plum (B), Lavender (C), Purple (D), Raspberry (E), Pink (F), Lilac (G) and Soft Green (H).
- 4mm (UK8:USG/6) crochet hook

Tension

Not crucial to this project.

Pattern notes

Make each flower-petal motif in a different colour combination of 7 colours.

Wrap

Using A, make a 2-finger wrap of 3 wraps (see page 44) or ch 7, sl st to complete round.

Round 1: Using A, 20 dc into the circle, sl st to complete round, cut off and weave in end (20 sts).

Round 2: Using B, attach yarn to any st, ch 2 (counts as tr), tr in next 3 sts, ch 5, *tr in next 4 sts, ch 5, repeat from * to end, sl st to complete round, cut and weave in end (5 loops).

Round 3: Using C, attach yarn in middle sp between any 4 tr of round 2, ch 1, (4 tr, ch 3, 4 tr) into the first loop, miss 2 sts, *dc in the sp before next st, miss 2 sts, (4 tr, ch 3, 4 tr) into the next loop, repeat from * to end, sl st to complete the round, cut and weave in end (5 petals).

Round 4: Using D, attach yarn at a petal point, ch 5, dtr into dc at dip of petal, ch 5, *dc in point, ch 5, dtr into dc at dip of petal, ch 5, repeat from * to end, sl st to complete round, cut and weave in end (10 loops).

Round 5: Continue using D, 6 dc into every ch 5 loop, sl st to complete round (60 dc).

Round 6: Continue using D, ch 4 (2 ch counts as tr, and 2 ch as sp), miss 1 st, *tr in next st, ch 2, miss 1 st, repeat from * to end, sl st to complete round (30 sp).

Round 7: Continue using D, 3 dc in every sp, sl st to complete round, cut and weave in end (90 sts).

Round 8: Using E, attach yarn in any st, ch 2 (counts as tr), tr in every st, sl st to complete round, cut and weave in end (90 sts).

Granny's tip

It doesn't matter which st you start in for rounds 9 and 10, but it is important that you start in the same st for each motif, so that the five petals are in the same position.

Round 9: Using F, 2 dc in first st, dc in next 8 sts, *2 dc in next st, dc in next 8 sts, repeat from * to end, sl st to complete round, cut and weave in end (100 sts).

Round 10: Using G, *dc in the next 6 sts, ch 7, dc in next 3 sts, ch 13, miss 1 st, dc in next 3 sts, ch 7, dc in next 6 sts, ch 3, dc in next 3 sts, ch 3, dc in next 3 sts, ch 3, repeat from * to end, sl st to complete round, cut and weave in end.

Join as you go for the chain loops

Round 10 is the join as you go round (see page 46). Match the same size ch loops to the next motif as you join corners and sides. A secondary pattern appears as you join the 4 corners together.

Ch 3 loops: Ch 1, ch 1 through the matching ch 3 loop, ch 1, to complete the ch 3 loops.

Ch 7 loops: Ch 3, ch 1 through the matching ch 7 loop, ch 3 to complete the ch 7 loops.

Ch 13 loops: Ch 6, ch 1 through the matching ch 13 loop, ch 6 to complete the ch 13 loops.

Finishing

Using H, join 2 rows of 10 motifs together to make the long wrap. You could add a third row of 10 motifs to make a deep wrap or make a shorter version with just 1 row of 4 motifs and join them into a circle for a cowl.

Drawstring

Using any colour, ch 4, sl st into a circle, 10 dc into circle, ch 74, sl st into the 4th ch from the hook, 10 dc into circle, sl st to complete, cut and weave in ends.

Thread through the ch loops, draw up and tie in a bow to hold.

Square ends
(alternative)

Pin out all the ch loops and press the wrap lightly.

Vintage-look Beret

This beret with a daisy-flower centre is made in the round in a lovely soft and snuggly alpaca. The project requires less than one ball of yarn to make and you could complete it in less than a day.

Finished size

10in (25cm) diameter. To fit small adult head 21–22in (53–56cm). Use larger hook to make a bigger size.

You will need

- Approximately 2oz (60g) in total of alpaca DK in 6 different colours (A–F in pattern).
  Version one (page 76): I used Olive (A), Lime (B), Red (C), Teal (D), Cinnamon (E), Toffee (F) in Stylecraft Alpaca DK to match collar, page 98.
  Version two (below): I used Teal (A), Lime (B), Cream (C), Toffee (D), Olive (E), Grey (F) in Stylecraft Alpaca DK.
- 4mm (UK8:USG/6) crochet hook

Tension

First 4 rounds of pattern measure 4in (10cm) diameter.

Pattern notes

This pattern uses half treble crochet. Yrh, insert hook into top two loops of next stitch in previous row, yrh. Pull yarn through stitch only (3 loops on hook), yrh, pull yarn through all 3 loops.

Beret

Using A, make a finger wrap of 4 wraps (see page 44) or ch 7, sl st to form a ring.

Round 1: Using A, ch 2 (counts as dc), 10 dc into wrap/circle, sl st to complete round, cut and weave in end (11 sts).

Round 2: Using B, attach yarn in any st, ch 2 (counts as dc, ch 1 sp), *dc in next st, ch 1, repeat from * to end, sl st to complete round, cut and weave in end (22 sts).

Round 3: Using C, attach yarn in any ch 1 sp, ch 3 (counts as dtr), 2 dtr cluster (see page 42) in same sp, *ch 3, 3 dtr cluster (see page 42) in next sp, repeat from * to end of round, ch 3, sl st to complete round, cut and weave in end (11 clusters).

Round 4: Using D, attach yarn in any sp, ch 2 (counts as tr), 3 tr in same sp, *ch 1, 4 dtr in next sp, repeat from * to end of round, ch 1, sl st to complete round, cut and weave in end (55 sts).

Round 5: Using E, attach yarn in any sp, ch 1 (counts as dc), ch 5, *dc in next sp, ch 5, repeat from * to end, sl st to complete round, cut and weave in end (11 loops).

Round 6: Using B, attach yarn in any loop, ch 2 (counts as tr), 5 tr in same loop, 6 tr in every loop to end, sl st to complete round, cut and weave in end (66 sts).

Round 7: Using E, attach yarn in top of first tr of round 6, ch 1 (counts as dc), dc in next 5 sts, dtr post st (see page 40) around dc of round 5, *dc in next 6 sts, dtr post st around dc of round 5, repeat from * to end of round, sl st to complete round, cut and weave in end (77 sts).

Round 8: Using F, attach yarn in any st, ch 2 (counts as tr), tr in every st, sl st to complete round, cut and weave in end (77 sts).

Round 9: Using C, attach yarn in st above the post st, ch 2 (counts as htr), htr in same st, htr in next 6 sts, *2 htr in next st, htr in next 6 sts* repeat to end, sl st to complete round, cut and weave in end (88 sts).

Round 10: Using D, attach yarn in second htr st, ch 2 (counts as tr), tr in same st, tr in next 3 sts, *2 tr in next st, tr in next 3 sts, repeat from * to end, sl st to complete round, cut and weave in end (110 sts).

Round 11: Using B, attach yarn on the first of a pair of sts of round 10, ch 2 (counts as tr), tr in next 2 sts, ch 3, miss 2 sts, *tr in next 3 sts, ch 3, miss 2 sts, repeat to end, sl st to complete round, cut and weave in end (22 loops).

Vintage-look Beret

Round 12: Using C, attach yarn in top of first st of any group of 3 sts, ch 1 (counts as dc), dc in next 2 sts, dc into loop, tr over the ch loop into next 2 missed sts of round 10, dc in next 3 sts, dc into loop, tr over the ch loop into next 2 missed sts of round 10, repeat from * to end, sl st to complete round, cut and weave in end (132 sts).

Round 13: Using F, attach yarn in any st, ch 1 (counts as dc), dc in every st, sl st to complete round, cut and weave in end (132 sts).

Round 14: Using E, attach yarn in any st, ch 2 (counts as tr), 2 tr in same st, miss 2 sts, *3 tr in next st, miss 2 sts, repeat from * to end, sl st to complete round, cut and weave in end (44 granny shells).

Round 15: Using B, attach yarn in any st, ch 2 (counts as tr), tr in every st, sl st to complete round, cut and weave in end (132 sts).

Round 16: Using E, attach yarn in any st, ch 1 (counts as dc), dc in every st, sl st to complete round, cut and weave in end (132 sts).

Round 17: Using B, attach yarn in any st, ch 2 (counts as tr), tr in next st, *tr 2 tog, tr in next 2 sts, repeat from * to end, sl st to complete round, cut and weave in end (99 sts).

Round 18: Using E, repeat round 16 (99 sts).

Round 19: Using B, repeat round 15 (99 sts).

Round 20: Using E, repeat round 16 (99 sts).

Round 21: Using B, repeat round 17, to last 3 sts, tr in each st (75 sts).

Round 22: Using E, repeat round 16 (75 sts).

Round 23: Using B, attach yarn in any st, ch 2 (counts as tr), *tr in next 13 sts, tr2 tog, repeat from * to end, sl st to complete round, cut and weave in end (70 sts).

Rounds 24–29: Continue using B, ch 1 (counts as dc), dc in every st, using a st marker to mark the last st, continue until 6 rounds have been completed, sl st into next st, cut and weave in end (70 sts).

granny's tip

When you are making a project in the round and you don't want to see the join for each round, use a spiral stitch, as used for the final band of this beret.

Beanie Bowl

This versatile granny pattern is quick to make, and looks very jolly made up in a rainbow of leftover cotton yarns. This handy little bowl is excellent for tidying away bits and pieces.

Finished size

Bowl circumference 21in (53.5cm)

You will need

- Approximately 1¾oz (50g) in total of cotton DK in 9 colours (A–J in pattern). I used warm yellow (A), white (B), green (C), turquoise (D), orange (E), pink (F), red (G), blue (H) and lemon yellow (J).
- 4mm (UK8:USG/6) crochet hook
- 7in (18cm)-diameter plastic bowl
- PVA glue and plastic wrap

Tension

First 4 rounds of pattern measure 4in (10cm) diameter.

Bowl

Using A, make a magic circle (see page 44) or ch 4, sl st into a circle.

Round 1: Using A, ch 2 (counts as a tr), 9 tr into the circle, sl st to complete round, cut and weave in end (10 sts).

Round 2: Using B, attach yarn in any st, ch 2 (counts as tr), 1 tr into same st, 2 tr into next st, ch 3, *2 tr in next 2 sts, ch 3, repeat from * to end, sl st to complete round, cut and weave in end (5 petals).

Round 3: Using C, attach yarn in any sp, ch 2 (counts as tr), (2 tr, ch 2, 3 tr, ch 2) into first sp, *(3 tr, ch 2, 3 tr, ch 2) into next sp, repeat from * to end, cut and weave in end (5 pairs of leaf granny shells).

Round 4: Using B, attach yarn in any sp, ch 2 (counts as tr), (2 tr, ch 1, 3 tr) in same sp, ch 1, *(3 tr, ch 1, 3 tr) in next sp, ch 1, repeat from * to end, cut and weave in end (10 pairs of granny shells).

Round 5: Using D, attach yarn in any sp, ch 2 (counts as dc) 2 tr in same sp, *3 tr in next sp, repeat from * to end, cut and weave in end (20 granny shells).

Rounds 6–15: Repeat round 5, in following colour sequence: B, E, B, F, B, G, B, H, B, J. Cut and weave in ends for each round (20 granny shells).

Finishing

To shape the bowl, cover the outside of the plastic bowl with plastic wrap. Cover your crocheted piece in PVA glue and mould it over the plastic bowl. Leave until it is completely dry, then gently pull your crochet bowl off the mould. If the bowl is still damp on the inside, leave it to dry for another day before use.

Granny's tip

If you leave the bowl unstiffened it makes a cute hat for a child.

Cami Top

This colourful sun top is perfect for a festival or a beach
holiday. Adjustable tie straps and the open join at the back
make it easy to wear. The rippled bottom edge means
it is easy to make the top whatever length you prefer.

Finished size
To fit UK size 8–12/US size 4–8

You will need
- 8¼oz (235g) in total of cotton DK in several colours. Each diamond is made with three colours (A–C in pattern). I used Stylecraft Classique DK yarn.
- 4mm (UK8:USG/6) crochet hook

Tension
Each motif measures 4½ x 3½in (11.5 x 9cm).

Pattern notes
Make each round of the diamonds in a different colour, using round 3 as the joining round (see page 46). Follow the chart for joining the diamonds together.

Granny's tip

You could repeat round 2 of the bottom edge until you've made this top into a pretty mini-dress.

Diamonds (make 44)
Using A, make a finger wrap of 4 wraps (see page 44), or ch 5, sl st to join into a ring.

Round 1: Using A, ch 2 (counts as 1 tr), 11 tr into circle, sl st to complete round, cut and weave in end (12 sts).

Round 2: Using B, attach yarn in any st, ch 3 (counts as 1 dtr), (1 dtr, ch 3, 2 dtr) into same st, 1 tr in next 2 sts, (2 tr, ch 2, 2 tr) into next st, 1 tr into next 2 sts, (2 dtr, ch 3, 2 dtr) into next st, 1 tr into next 2 sts, (2 tr, ch 2, 2 tr) into next st, 1 tr in next 2 sts, sl st to complete, cut and weave in end (6 sts each side).

Round 3: Using C, attach yarn in a ch 3 sp, ch 3 (counts as 1 dtr), (1 dtr, ch 3, 2 dtr) into same ch sp, tr into next 6 sts, (1 tr, ch 2, 1 tr) into next ch sp, 1 tr in next 6 sts, (2 dtr, ch 3, 2 dtr) in next ch sp, 1 tr in next 6 sts, (1 tr, ch 2, 1 tr) in next ch sp, 1 tr in next 6 sts, sl st to complete, cut and weave in ends (9 sts each side).

Making up
Front: Following the chart, join as you go in every stitch or stitch together the front (20 diamonds).

Back: Join as you go in the points (sides, top and bottom) of each diamond only (20 diamonds). By only joining the points you create an additional stretch to the back, allowing a multi-size fit.

Sides: Join last 4 diamonds to form sides.

Strap (make 2)

Use 2 colours to create a narrow strap with ring ends.

Front

Make a finger wrap of 4 wraps (see page 44) or ch 5, sl st to join into a ring. Ch 1 (counts as 1 dc), 9 dc into circle, ch 50 (strap), *2 dc into first ch sp (top of diamond), 1 dc in next 9 sts, 1 dc into ch sp, 1 dc into joining st, 1 dc into ch sp, 1 dc into next 9 sts, 1 dc into ch sp, 1 dc into joining st, 1 dc into next ch sp, 1 dc into next 9 sts, 1 dc into joining st, 1 dc into ch sp, 1 dc into next 9 sts, 2 dc into last ch sp*, ch 55, ch 5 (to make end ring) sl st into the 5th stitch from hook, 10 dc into circle, sl st to complete, cut and weave in end.

Back

Repeat as front.

Armholes

Using a different colour, 2 dc into each st around one of the front strap rings, miss first 2 sts of strap, 1 dc in every ch, repeat as for Front strap from * to * along underarm edge, 1 dc in next 48 sts, 2 dc in each st of second ring, sl st to complete. Cut and weave in end.
Repeat on second armhole.

Bottom edge

Round 1: Starting in a dip, attach yarn in first sp, 1 dc in same sp, 1 dc in next 9 sts, (2 dc, ch 1, 2 dc) in point, 1 dc in next 9 sts, 1 dc in sp, miss joining st, *1 dc in next sp, 1 dc in next 9 sts, (2 dc, ch 1, 2 dc) in point, 1 dc in next 9 sts, 1 dc in sp, miss joining st, repeat from * for all points, sl st to complete.

Round 2: Start in the second st from start of dip, *1 dc in 11 sts, (1 dc, ch 1, 1 dc) in point, 1 dc in next 11 sts, miss 2 sts, repeat from * for all points, sl st to complete, cut and weave in end.

Round 3: Repeat round 2.

If you need extra length, repeat round 2 until garment is the length required, changing colour for each round.

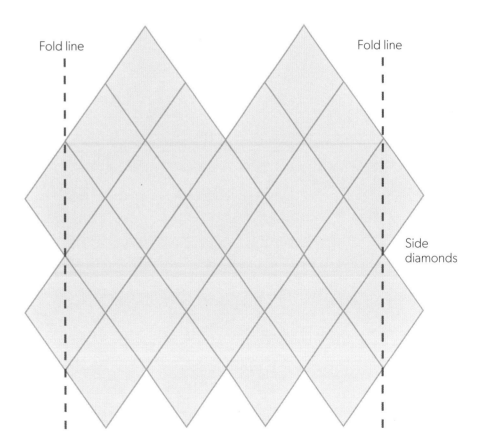

Fold line   Fold line

Side diamonds

Front and back diamonds

Shawl Pin

This shawl pin can be made in minutes from tiny scraps
of yarn – use one yarn or different colours for each round.
You can add chain stitch to the middle of the motif for added
detail if you like. It also makes a great hair ornament.

Finished size

5 x 4in (12.5 x 10cm)

You will need

- Approximately ½oz (12g) in total in 3 colours (A–C in pattern) of cotton or other yarns. I used Noro yarn.
- 4mm (UK8:USG/6) crochet hook
- Hair chopstick as pin
- Bowl or cardboard tube for shaping
- PVA glue

Tension

Not crucial to this project.

Shawl pin

Using A, make a magic circle (see page 44) or ch 4, sl st into a circle.

Round 1: Using A, ch 2 (counts as tr), 11 tr into circle, sl st to complete round, cut and weave in ends (12 tr).

Round 2: Using B, ch 3 (counts as ttr), 2 ttr cluster into same st, ch 3, *3 ttr cluster (see page 42) into next st, ch 3, repeat from * to end, sl st to complete round, cut and weave in ends (12 clusters).

Round 3: Using C, ch 2 (counts as tr), 3 tr in same sp, ch 3, 4 tr in next sp (this is the first end), 4 tr in each of the next 5 sp, ch 3, 4 tr in each of next 5 sp, sl st to complete round, cut and weave in end (48 tr, 2 x ch 3 ends for the pin).

Alternative centre
(pictured on page 89)

Round 1: Using A, make a 2-finger wrap of 3 wraps (see page 44) or ch 7, sl st into a circle.

Round 2: Ch 1 (counts as dc), 11 dc into circle, sl st to complete round, cut off and weave in end (12 dc). Work rounds 2 and 3 from original design.

Finishing

Stiffen the shawl pin by applying a strong solution of PVA glue and leave it to dry for a day in a warm place, moulded over a bowl or cardboard tube to give it a gentle curved shape.

Daisy Top

This wonderfully simple and easy-to-wear daisy-inset top is made up of granny squares with a twist. The front and back are identical, and the underarm and shoulder triangles create the perfect one-size shape.

Finished size

To fit UK size 10–16/US size 6–12

You will need

- 14oz (400g) in total of cotton DK in a selection of colours
- 2–2½oz (60–70g) cotton DK in black (A)
- Small quantity of cotton DK in cream (B)
- Small quantity of cotton DK in yellow (C)
  I used Stylecraft Classique Cotton DK.
- 4mm (UK8:USG/6) crochet hook

Pattern notes

Each round of the granny squares is in your choice of colour from your selection, except where specified. Join 18 granny squares together for the front and 18 for the back. Inset 4 daisy motifs into the holes. Make 4 granny squares and 4 triangles to join the front to the back, by folding them in half, following the diagram.

Tension

Not crucial to this project.

Granny square
(make 40)

Round 1: Ch 2 (counts as 1 tr), 2 tr, ch 2, 3 tr, ch 2, 3 tr, ch 2, 3 tr, ch 2, sl st to complete, cut and weave in end (4 granny shells).

Round 2: Attach yarn in any ch sp, ch 2 (counts as 1 tr), (2 tr, ch 2, 3 tr) into same ch sp, ch 1, *(3 tr, ch 2, 3 tr) into next sp, ch 1, repeat from * to end, sl st to complete, cut and weave in end (8 granny shells).

Round 3: Attach yarn in any ch 2 corner sp, *3 dtr, ch 3, 3 dtr into next ch 1 side sp, dc into next ch 2 corner sp, repeat from * to end, finish with a sl st to complete, cut and weave in end.

Round 4: Attach yarn in a corner sp, ch 2 (counts as a tr), (1 tr, ch 2, 2 tr) into same sp, 1 tr in next 7 sts, *(2 tr, ch 2, 2 tr) in next corner sp, 1 tr in next 7 sts, repeat from * to end, sl st to complete, cut and weave in ends.

Joining round

Round 5: Using A, attach yarn in a corner sp, ch 3 (counts as 1 tr and ch 1 sp), 1 tr into same corner sp, ch 1, miss 1 st, *1 tr into next st, ch 1, miss 1 st, repeat from * to next corner sp, (1 tr, ch 1, 1 tr, ch 3, 1 tr, ch 1, 1 tr) into corner sp, ch 1, miss 1 st, repeat from * to end, sl st to complete, cut and weave in end. When joining use a slip st in every ch sp.

Underarm and neck triangle (make 4)

Make a magic circle or ch 4, sl st into a circle.

Round 1: Ch 2 (counts as 1 tr), 2 tr, ch 3, 3 tr, ch 3, 3 tr, ch 3, sl st to complete, cut and weave in end (3 granny shells).

Round 2: Attach yarn in any ch sp, ch 2 (counts as 1 tr), (2 tr, ch 3, 3 tr) into same sp, ch 2, *(3 tr, ch 3, 3 tr) into next ch sp, ch 2, repeat from * to end, sl st to complete, cut and weave in end (6 granny shells).

Round 3: Attach yarn in any corner ch 3 sp, ch 2 (counts as 1 tr), (2 tr, ch 3, 3 tr) into same sp, ch 1, *3 tr into next ch sp, ch 1, (3 tr, ch 3, 3 tr) in next corner sp, ch 1, repeat from * to end, sl st to complete, cut and weave in end (9 granny shells).

Joining round

Round 4: Using A, attach yarn in any corner sp, ch 3 (counts as 1 tr and ch 1 sp), 1 tr into same sp, *ch 1, miss 1 st, 1 tr into next st, ch 1, miss 1 st, 1 tr into next ch sp, repeat from * to next corner sp, miss 1 st, (1 tr, ch 1, 1 tr, ch 3, 1 tr, ch 1, 1 tr) into corner sp, ch 1, miss 1 st, repeat from * to end, finishing with (1 tr, ch 1, 1 tr, ch 3) into last corner sp, sl st to complete, cut and weave in end. When joining use a sl st into every ch sp.

Daisy motif (make 4)

Using C, make a finger wrap of 4 wraps (see page 44) or ch 6, sl st into a circle.

Round 1: Continue using C, ch 2 (counts as 1 tr), 15 tr into circle, sl st to complete, cut and weave in end (16 sts).

Round 2: Using B, attach yarn in any st, ch 2 (counts as 1 tr), 1 tr into same st, ch 6, *2 tr into next 2 sts, ch 6, repeat from * to end, finishing with 2 tr in last st, sl st to complete, do not cut yarn (8 ch loops).

Joining (inset) round

Round 3: Continue using B, *(4 tr, ch 3, 4 tr) into next ch 6 sp, miss 2 sts, dc into sp before next st, miss 2 sts, repeat from * to end, sl st to complete, cut and weave in end (8 petals).

Finishing

Add 4 rows of dc around neck, 2 rows around armholes and bottom points.

Neck

Round 1: Using A, starting at the back dip, attach yarn in first ch sp, ch 1 (counts as 1 dc), 1 dc in next sp, *2 dc in next 6 ch sp (side of a granny square), 1 dc in next 4 ch sp (joined corners of granny square), repeat from * to front dip, miss the joining st, repeat on other side of neck, missing the last joining st (64 sts).

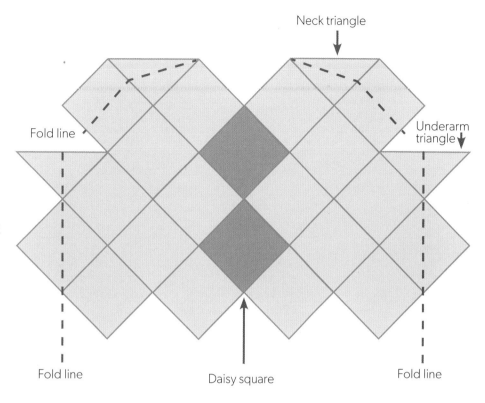

Neck triangle

Fold line

Underarm triangle

Fold line

Daisy square

Fold line

Round 2: 1 dc in every st, missing 2 sts at front and back dips in neck line. This will keep the neckline flat.

Rounds 3–4: Repeat round 1 but miss 1 st at the shoulder on both sides, so the garment curves slightly.

Armholes

Round 1: Using A, starting at bottom right of armhole, attach yarn in first ch sp, ch 1 (counts as 1 dc), 1 dc in same sp, 2 dc in next 9 ch sps, miss 1 ch sp, 2 dc in next 27 ch sps, miss 1 ch sp, sl st to complete.

Round 2: 1 dc in every st. Repeat for second armhole.

Bottom

Round 1: Using A, starting in a dip, attach yarn in first st, ch 1 (counts as 1 dc), *2 dc in next 8 ch sp, (2 dc, ch 2, 2 dc) in point, 2 dc in next 8 ch sp, 1 dc in next sp, miss 1 st, repeat from * for each point, sl st to complete.

Round 2: 1 dc in each st, miss 2 sts at dip, work (2 dc, ch 2, 2 dc) at points.

Bright Collar

This collar can be made in cotton to brighten up a plain T-shirt in summer or cashmere to add luxury to a winter jumper. This smaller version with a flower decoration (left) was made in alpaca to match the Vintage-look Beret on page 76.

Finished size

Cashmere collar 3½in (9cm) deep, centre diameter 10in (25cm); cotton collar 5in (12cm) deep, centre diameter 9in (23cm); smaller collar 4½in (11cm) deep, centre diameter 6in (15cm)

You will need

Cashmere collar

- Approximately 2½–3oz (70–90g) of cashmere yarn in one colour or small quantities of 6 different colours (A–F in pattern). I used ColourMart Cashmere in Lilac (A), Orange (B), Pink (C), Dark Red (D), Yellow (E) and Golden Yellow (F).
- 4mm (UK8:USG/6) crochet hook

Cotton collar

- Approximately 2½–3oz (70–90g) of cotton or cotton bamboo yarn in one colour or small quantities of 8 different colours (A–H in pattern). I used Stylecraft Classique Cotton and King Cole Bamboo Cotton in Shrimp (A), Hot Pink (B), Poppy (C), Lavender (D), Plum (E), Warm Pink (F), Seville (G) and Olive Green (H).
- 4mm (UK8:USG/6) crochet hook

Smaller collar (to match beret on page 76)

- Approximately 3–3½oz (80–100g) in total of alpaca yarn in the same colours as the beret in any combination. I used Stylecraft Alpaca DK in Red, Lime, Cinnamon, Toffee, Teal and Olive.
- 4mm (UK8:USG/6) crochet hook

Flower decoration

- Small quantities of alpaca yarn. I used Stylecraft Alpaca DK in Olive (A) and Lime (B).
- 4mm (UK8:USG/6) crochet hook

Tension

Not crucial to this project.

Cashmere collar

Cotton collar

Cashmere and cotton collars

Using A, ch 112 (be careful not to twist the long chain), sl st into a circle.

Round 1: Using A, ch 2 (counts as a tr), tr in next 3 sts, ch 1, *tr in next 4 sts, ch 1, repeat from * to end of round, sl st to complete round, cut off and weave in end (140 sts; 112 tr, 28 ch sp).

Round 2: Using B, attach yarn in any ch 1 sp, ch 1 (counts as dc), ch 4, *dc in next sp, ch 4, repeat from * to end, sl st to complete round, cut and weave in end (28 loops).

Round 3: Using C, attach yarn in any loop, ch 2 (counts as tr), 5 tr into loop, *6 tr in next loop, repeat from * to end, sl st to complete round, cut and weave in end (168 sts).

Round 4: Using D, attach yarn in any sp, ch 1 (counts as dc), ch 6, *dc in next sp, ch 6, repeat from * to end, sl st to complete round, cut and weave in end (28 loops).

Round 5: Using E, attach yarn in any loop, ch 2 (counts as tr), 6 tr in same loop, *7 tr in next loop, repeat from * for all loops, sl st to complete round, cut and weave in end (196 sts).

Round 6: Using B, attach yarn in any first st of a group of 7 tr, ch 3 (counts as dtr), 3 dtr cluster in next st (see page 42), ch 3, miss 2 sts, 4 dtr cluster in next st, ch 3, miss 3 sts, *4 dtr cluster in next st, ch 3, miss 2 sts, 4 dtr cluster in next st, ch 3, miss 3 sts, repeat from * to end, sl st to complete round, cut and weave in end (56 clusters).

Round 7: Using F, attach yarn in any sp, ch 1 (counts as dc), htr, tr, dtr, ttr into same sp, ch 2, ttr, dtr, tr, htr, dc, into next sp, *dc, htr, tr, dtr, ttr into next sp, ch 2, ttr, dtr, tr, htr, dc into next sp, repeat from * to end, sl st to complete round, cut and weave in end (28 points).

Cotton collar only

Round 8: Using G, attach yarn in any point, ch 1 (counts as dc), ch 7, *dc in next sp, ch 7, repeat from * to end, sl st to complete round (28 loops).

Round 9: Continue with G, ch 2 (counts as tr), 8 tr into same loop, *9 tr into next loop, repeat from * to end, sl st to complete round, cut and weave in end (252 sts).

Round 10: Using H, attach yarn in first st of 9 tr, *miss 2 sts, 5 tr into next st, miss 2 sts, sl st into next st, repeat from * to end, sl st to complete round (42 shells).

Smaller collar

To make a smaller collar (like this one in alpaca to match the beret on page 76), remove multiples of 8 sts. Remove up to a maximum of 16 base ch st for a close fitting, adult collar. Small adult collar 96 ch, medium 104 ch, large 112 ch.

Flower decoration

Stem: Using A, make a finger wrap of 3 wraps (see page 44), ch 1 (counts as dc), 11 dc into circle, sl st to complete ring (12 sts), *ch 15, 12 dc into 2nd st from the hook (6 sts one side of the long ch and 6 sts on the other), sl st to start of ring, repeat from * 3 more times.

Flowers (make 5): Using B, attach yarn in any st of a ring, *ch 2, tr in same st, (tr, ch 2, sl st) into next st, sl st into the next st, repeat from * to end, sl st to complete round, cut off and weave in ends (6 petals).

Finishing

Thread the middle flower through one of the stitches and tie on. Weave the next two flowers through the collar and leave the end flowers to hang.

Mini Bag

This humbug-shaped mini bag is made from two striped solid granny squares, decorated with Japanese flowers. You can make a cute purse to go with it from just one square. The bag is secured with a zip, while the purse has a little drawstring.

Finished size

Bag 6¾ x 6¼in (17 x 16cm); purse 4½in (11cm) square

You will need

- 3oz (85g) in total of cotton DK yarn in 10 different colours. I used Stylecraft Classique Cotton DK in Black (A), Hot Pink (B), Cream (C), Wisteria (D), Soft Lime (E), Shrimp (F) and Seville (G) for the bag and purse. For the flowers I used combinations of Seville, Sunflower, Lavender and Poppy.
- 4mm (UK8:USG/6) crochet hook
- 6in (15cm) zip
- Yarn needle

Tension

Not crucial to this project.

Granny square for bag (make 2)

Using A, make a finger wrap of 4 wraps (see page 44) or ch 5, sl st into a circle.

Round 1: Using A, ch 1 (counts as 1 dc), 15 dc into circle, sl st to complete, pull yarn through st, do not cut off (16 sts).

Round 2: Using B, attach yarn in any st, ch 1 (counts as 1 dc), ch 2, 1 dc into same st, 1 dc into next 3 sts, *(1 dc, ch 2, 1 dc) into next st, 1 dc into next 3 sts, repeat from * to end, sl st to complete, cut and weave in end.

Round 3: Using A, repeat round 2 with an increase of 2 sts on each side. Start in a corner sp.

Rounds 4–15: Repeat round 3, alternating colours C, D, C, E, C, F with main colour A.

Making up

Stitch the zip between the two squares. Using A, work dc, matching the stitches on both squares, across the top and down the 3rd side. Flatten the sides so that the zip is central, and the bottom is at right angles to the top seam. Stitch or dc the last two sides together, making a humbug shape.

Strap

Using A, attach yarn to the top of the bag above the top of the closed zip, ch 70, sl st to the bag making a long loop, return along the ch 70, working 1 dc in every st, sl st to complete, cut and securely stitch in ends (70 sts).

Fastening loop

Using A, attach yarn to the corner opposite the side with the zip, ch 12, sl st close to the start of the ch 12, 1 dc in every st, sl st to complete, cut and sew in ends securely (12 sts).

The bag can be left as a humbug shape or folded flat by threading the long strap through the small loop.

Flowers (make 6 in different colour combinations)

Round 1: Using any of the colours, make a finger wrap of 4 wraps, ch 1 (counts as 1 dc), 11 dc into circle, sl st to complete round, cut and weave in end (12 sts).

Round 2: Using a different colour, attach yarn in any st, ch 2 (counts as tr), tr into same st, 2 tr into every st, sl st to complete round, cut and weave in end (24 sts).

Finishing

Stitch 2 flowers to each side of the bag with a double strand of yarn in a contrasting colour. Stitch up between the inner circle and outer circle of flower (from inside the bag), then down slightly under the outer edge of the circle, using each pair of treble sts as a guide.

Matching purse

Rounds 1–15: Work as for bag, using G instead of F in round 15.

Making up

Fold the 4 corners towards the centre. Using F, stitch or crochet the edges for about 10 sts from the outer corner, leaving the remaining sts open.

Drawstring

Using F, make a finger wrap of 4 wraps or ch 5, sl st into a circle. Ch 1 (counts as 1 dc), 9 dc into circle, sl st to complete round, ch 75, thread the drawstring through all the points of the purse, sl st into 5th st from hook, 10 dc into circle, sl st to complete, cut and weave in end.

Finishing

Decorate with 4 flowers following the pattern and instructions for the mini bag.

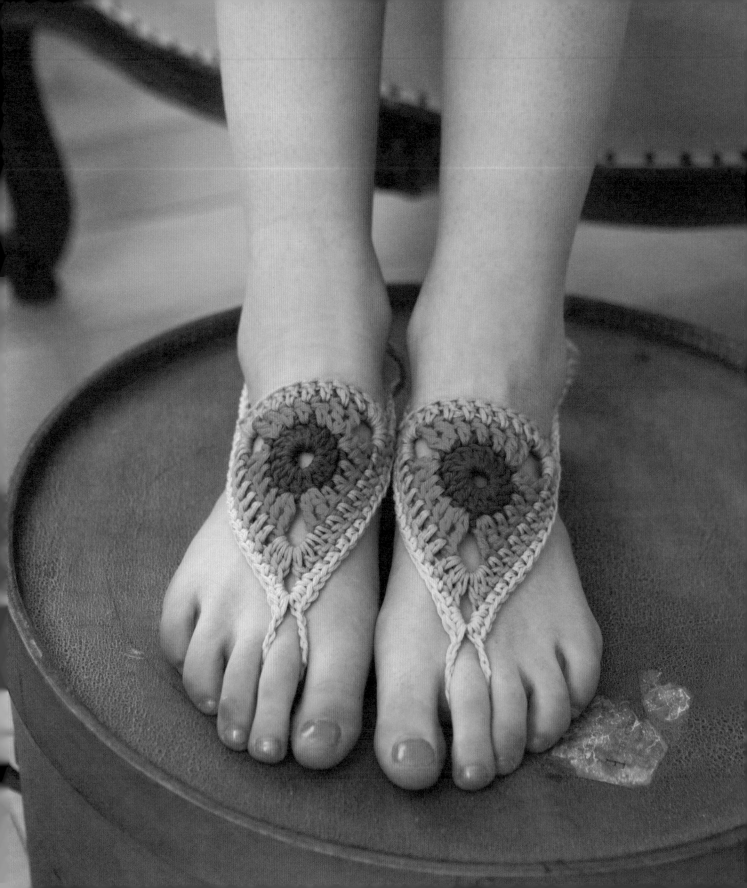

Foot Decoration

This foot decoration is a quick project, ideal for using up any tiny balls of cotton you might have left over. Use this colourful decoration to decorate plain sandals or even your bare feet and hands.

Finished size

Sides of triangle 4in (10cm)

You will need

- Approximately ½–¾oz (15–20g) in total of cotton yarn in 4 colours of your choice (A–D in pattern). I used oddments of Stylecraft Classique Cotton DK and King Cole Bamboo Cotton.
- 4mm (UK8:USG/6) crochet hook

Tension

Not crucial to this project.

Foot decoration
(make 2)

Using A, make a finger wrap of 4 wraps (see page 44) or ch 4, sl st into a circle.

Round 1: Using A, ch 2 (counts as tr), 14 tr into circle, sl st to complete, cut and weave in ends (15 sts).

Round 2: Using B, attach yarn in any st, ch 3 (counts as dtr), dtr into same st, tr into next 3 sts, 2 dtr into next st, ch 4, *2 dtr in next st, tr in next 3 sts, 2 dtr in next st, ch 4, repeat from * to end, sl st to complete round, cut and weave in end (11 sts each side including ch).

Round 3: Using C, attach yarn in any sp, ch 2 (counts as tr), (2 tr, ch 3, 3 tr) into same sp, tr in next 7 sts, *(3 tr, ch 3, 3 tr) into next sp, tr in next 7 sts, repeat from * to end, sl st to complete round, cut and weave in end (16 sts each side including ch).

Round 4 and ties: Using D, ch 5, sl st to make a circle, 10 dc into circle, ch 50, 3 dc into any corner sp, dc in next 13 sts, (3 dc, ch 12, 3 dc) into next corner sp (toe loop), dc into next 13 sts, 3 dc into last corner sp, ch 55, sl st into 5th ch from hook, 10 dc into circle, sl st to complete, cut and weave in end (19 dc on two sides).

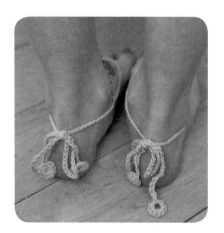

Granny's tip

You could add flowers to the tie ends to create a more decorative look.

Heart Bunting

These simple granny hearts can be made in one colour with no decoration or in several colours and decorated with circles or flowers. You can make the bunting as long or as short as you like. The choice is yours!

Finished size

Each heart measures 3¼in (8.25cm) at the widest point.

You will need

- Approximately 1⅜oz (40g) cotton DK in main colour (A) for a 6-heart garland. Small quantities of other colours for edging (B), hanging rings (C) and petals (D).
- 4mm (UK8:USG/6) crochet hook

Tension

Each heart measures 3¼in (8.25cm) in diameter. Use larger or smaller needles if necessary to obtain correct tension.

Pattern notes

For a crisp finish, use Stylecraft Classique Cotton or Freedom Sincere Organic Cotton. For a softer finish, use Bamboo Cotton.

Basic granny heart

(make 6)

Using A, make a finger wrap of 3 wraps (see page 44) or ch 5, sl st into a circle.

Round 1: Using A, ch 2 (counts as 1 tr), 2 tr, ch 2, *3 tr, ch 2, repeat from * twice more, do not join into a square, turn (4 granny shells).

Round 2: Continue using A, (3 tr, ch 2, 3 tr) into first ch 2 sp, ch 1, (3 tr, ch 2, 3 tr) into bottom point of heart, ch 1, (3 tr, ch 2, 3 tr) into next ch 2 sp, ch 2, sl st into first st of round 1, turn (6 granny shells).

Round 3: Continue using A, ch 2, 3 tr into first ch 2 sp, ch 2, 3 tr into next ch 2 sp, ch 2, 3 tr into next ch 1 sp, ch 1, (3 tr, ch 2, 3 tr) into point of heart, ch 1, 3 tr into next ch 1 sp, ch 2, 3 tr into next ch 2 sp, ch 2, 3 tr into last ch 2 sp, ch 2, sl st into first st of round 2, cut and weave in ends (8 granny shells).

Outer edging

Using B, add a round of dc, with 2 dc in each of the top three tr on both sides of the heart, so that the heart tops do not curl.

Joining together

Using C, make a finger wrap of 3 wraps or ch 5, sl st into a circle.

Round 1 (hanging ring): 10 dc into the circle, sl st to complete round. To join hearts together, ch 10, dc into the first highest st of the heart top, ch 8 between the heart sides, dc into the highest st of the second heart top, ch 10 between each heart, repeat to join all the hearts together, ch 10.

To make the second hanging ring, ch 5, sl st into the 5th st from the hook.

Round 1: 10 dc into the circle, sl st to complete, cut and weave in end.

Flowers

Using C, make a finger wrap of 3 wraps or ch 5, sl st into a circle.

Round 1: Using C, 10 dc into the circle, sl st to complete round.

Round 2: Using D, *ch 2, tr into first st, (tr, ch 2, sl st) into second st, repeat from * to end for 5 petals, sl st to complete round, cut and weave in end.

Finishing

You can embellish your bunting as much or as little as you like. Decorate the hearts with rings at the bottom points using the same pattern as the hanging rings, or make flowers and stitch them to the hearts.

Granny's tip

For an individual heart decoration, make a flower hanger by adding a chain loop to a flower and threading it through the top of the heart.

Colourful Dish

Use this pretty granny circle design to make a colourful shallow dish, stiffened with PVA glue. This is a great project for using up leftover yarn. You can create some table mats using the same pattern to make a matching set.

Finished size

Smaller dish 9½in (24cm) diameter; larger dish 12in (30cm) diameter

You will need

Smaller dish

- Approximately 1¾oz (50g) in total of cotton DK in 7 colours (A–G in pattern). I used grey (A), white (B), bright pink (C), lime green (D), red (E), mint green (F) and jade (G).
- 7½in (19cm)-diameter bowl
- 4mm (UK8:USG/6) crochet hook
- PVA glue and plastic wrap

Larger dish

- Approximately 2oz (60g) in total of cotton DK in 7 colours (A–G in pattern). I used orange (A), lemon yellow (B), ochre (C), melon (D), burgundy (E), lavender (F) and purple (G).
- 7½in (19cm)-diameter bowl
- 5mm (UK6:USH/8) crochet hook
- PVA glue and plastic wrap

Tension

Not crucial to this project.

Dish

Using A, make a finger wrap of 3 wraps (see page 44) or ch 4, sl st into a circle.

Round 1: Using A, ch 2 (counts as tr), 15 tr into circle, sl st to complete round, cut and weave in end (16 tr).

Round 2: Using B, attach yarn in any st, ch 3 (counts as dtr), dtr in same st, 2 dtr cluster in next st, ch 4, * 2 dtr cluster in the next 2 sts, ch 4, repeat from * to end, sl st to complete round, cut and weave in end (8 petals).

Round 3: Using C, attach yarn in any sp, ch 3 (counts as tr), 4 tr in same sp, ch 2, *5 tr in next sp, ch 2, repeat from * to end, sl st to complete round, cut and weave in end (8 x 5 tr granny shells).

Round 4: Using D, attach yarn in any sp, ch 3 (counts as dtr), 2 dtr in same sp, miss 2 sts, 3 dtr in next st, miss 2 sts, *3 dtr in next sp, miss 2 sts, 3 dtr in next st, miss 2 sts, repeat from * to end, sl st to complete round, cut and weave in end (16 granny shells).

Round 5: Using E, attach yarn in first tr of any granny shell, ch 2 (counts as tr), tr in next 2 sts, tr in the sp, *tr in next 3 sts, tr in the sp, repeat from * to end, sl st to complete round, cut and weave in end (64 sts).

Round 6: Using F, attach yarn in any st, ch 3 (counts as dtr), dtr in next 3 sts, ch 3, *dtr in next 4 sts, ch 3, repeat from * to end, sl st to complete round, cut and weave in end (16 loops).

Granny's tip

Using the same yarn but with a slightly bigger hook means the dish will be a little lacier and slightly larger.

Larger dish

Smaller dish

granny's tip

Use the same pattern to make matching mats. You can stiffen the mat in the same way as the bowl and leave it to dry flat. Or leave it unstiffened for a soft mat.

Round 7: Using G, attach yarn in any loop, ch 2 (counts as tr), (2tr, ch 3, 3tr) in same loop, miss 2 sts, dc into sp before next st, *miss 2 sts, (3 tr, ch 3, 3 tr) into next loop, miss 2 sts, dc into sp before next st, repeat from * to end, sl st to complete round, cut and weave in end (16 points).

Finishing

Cover the bowl in plastic wrap. Soak the crochet bowl in PVA glue. Stretch the crochet bowl over the wrap-covered bowl, pulling all the points to make them sharp. Ensure the pointed edges are even. Leave until dry and firm to the touch, then gently remove it from the mould. If the bowl is slightly damp inside, leave it to dry completely before use.

Triangle Lap Blanket

This fabulous lap blanket is made from super-soft triangles in delicious muted colours, joined together with little circles. The blanket is finished with an edging of small coloured circles for an extra touch of style.

Finished size

48 x 42in (121 x 106cm)

You will need

- 10 x 1¾oz (50g) balls 50% alpaca/50% merino yarn in base colour (A)
- 12 x 1¾oz (50g) balls 50% alpaca/50% merino yarn in 12 different colours.
  I used Rooster Almerino Aran in Cornish (base colour), Sugared Almond, Custard, Brighton, Hazelnut, Lolly, Lilac Sky, Shimmer, Sorbet, Sandcastle, Beach, Smoothie and Strawberry cream.
- 4.5mm (UK7:US7) crochet hook

Tension

Not crucial to this project.

Blanket motif
(make 96, 8 in each of the 12 colours)

Using A, make a finger wrap of 4 wraps (see page 44) or ch 5, sl st to complete round.

Round 1: Using A, ch 2 (counts as tr), 17 tr into circle, sl st to complete round, cut and weave in end (18 sts).

Round 2: Using selected colour, attach yarn in any st, ch 3 (counts as 1 dtr), 1 dtr into same st, * 1 tr into next 4 sts, 2 dtr into next st, ch 5, 2 dtr into next st, repeat from * to end, finishing with 2 dtr in last st, ch 5, sl st to complete round.

Round 3: Continue using selected colour, ch 2 (counts as 1 tr), 1 tr in next 7 sts, (3 tr, ch 3, 3 tr) in next ch 5 corner sp, *1 tr in next 8 sts, (3 tr, ch 3, 3 tr) in next ch 5 corner sp, repeat from * to end, sl st to complete, cut and weave in end (14 sts each side).

Join triangles

Lay out the triangles in a pleasing combination and join them together in rows, following the diagram, using a sl st in the ch 1 stitches on each of the triangle sides.

Round 1: Using A, attach yarn in a corner sp, ch 2 (counts as 1 tr), (1 tr, ch 2, 2 tr) into same sp, 1 tr into next 4 sts, ch 1, 1 tr into next 6 sts, ch 1, 1 tr into next 4 sts, *(2 tr, ch 2, 2 tr) into next corner sp, 1 tr into next 4 sts, ch 1, 1 tr into next 6 sts, ch 1, 1 tr into next 4 sts, repeat from * to end, sl st to complete round, cut and weave in end.

Using a sl st, join the triangles together at the 2 ch 1 sp only.

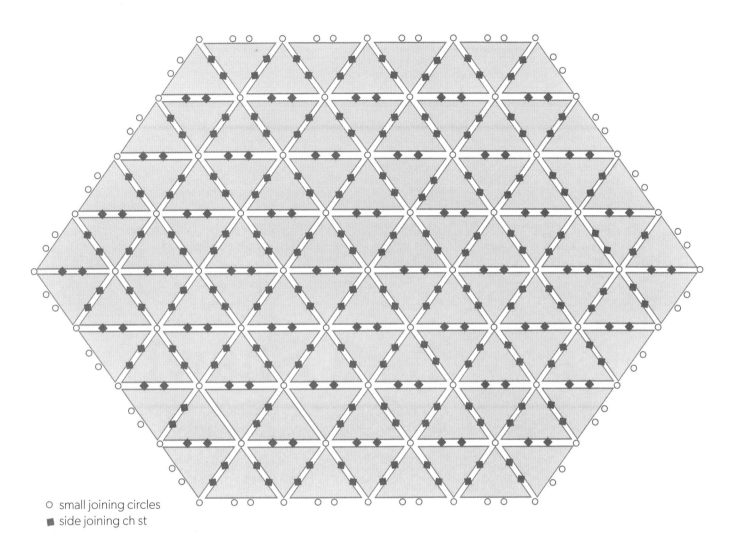

○ small joining circles
■ side joining ch st

Joining circles

Join the internal triangles together first, after joining 2 rows of triangles. Work on the outer edge joins after you have put the whole hexagon together. Using A, work a finger wrap of 4 wraps or ch 5, sl st to complete round.

Round 1: Continue using A, *2 dc into circle, sl st into a triangle point, repeat from * until 6 triangles are attached to the circle, sl st to complete, cut and weave in end (12 dc).

Finishing

Refer to the diagram. Using A, work a circle at each outer point where 3 triangles meet. Using a random selection of B–N, add 2 circles to each triangle on the ch 1 sts around the outer edge of hexagon.

Pinwheel Shawl

This soft, pretty shawl in a delightful lacy motif will work with any style of outfit, from evening dress to jeans. Each round is in a different colour and each motif is a different combination, giving a subtle and delicate effect.

Finished size

41in (104cm) at widest point

You will need

- 2 x 1¾oz (50g) balls 50% alpaca/ 50% merino yarn in the joining colour (A).
- 8 x 1¾oz (50g) balls 50% alpaca/ 50% merino yarn in 8 different colours used randomly. I used Rooster Almerino Aran in Cornish (joining colour), Strawberry Cream, Ocean, Hazelnut, Shimmer, Lolly and Sandcastle; Ella Rae Classic Heathers in Soft Jade; Ella Rae Classic in Lime
- 4.5mm (UK7:US7) crochet hook

Tension

Each motif measures approximately 5in (12.5cm). Use a larger or smaller hook if necessary to obtain correct tension.

Pattern notes

Use a mixture of three different colours (B–D) for each motif, plus the joining colour (A).

Granny's tip

You could arrange the motifs differently to make a long wrap.

Pinwheel motif

(make 33)

Using B, make a finger wrap of 3 wraps (see page 44) or ch 5 sl st into a circle.

Round 1: Using B, 12 dc into the circle, sl st to complete round, cut and weave in ends (12 sts).

Round 2: Using C, attach yarn in any st, ch 4 (counts as 1 tr and ch 2 sp), *tr into next st, ch 2, repeat from * to end, sl st to complete round, cut and weave in end (12 spokes).

Round 3: Using D, attach yarn in any ch sp, *ch 5, dc into next sp, repeat from * to end, sl st to complete round, cut and weave in end (12 ch loops).

Round 4: Using A, attach yarn in any st, ch 6, *dc into next loop, ch 6, repeat from * to end.

Round 5: Continue in A, 7 dc into first loop, repeat for each loop, sl st to complete round, cut and weave in end.

Finishing

Use the join as you go method (see page 46) on the 4th dc of each loop of Round 5, joining two loops to two loops on every side of hexagon. Join the motifs together in the pattern shown below to form a triangular shawl.

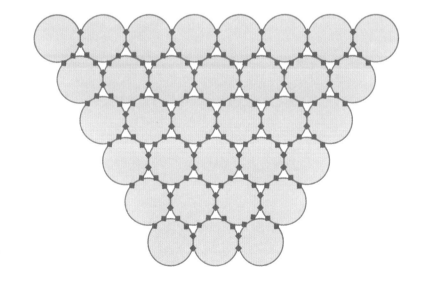

Black-edged Lace Mat

This lacy mat with pretty hexagonal flower motifs provides stylish protection for a table. Each round is in a different colour and each motif in a different combination, all encased in two rounds of black. Add matching coasters for a lovely set.

Granny's tip

Single motifs can be made into coasters by adding a round of 7 dc after round 3. On the last round use 7 dc.

Finished size

19½in (50cm) long

You will need

- Approximately 1¾oz (50g) in total of cotton DK yarn in a variety of bright colours and black (D)
- 4mm (UK8:USG/6) crochet hook

Tension

Not crucial to this project.

Pattern notes

Use a mixture of three different colours (A–C in pattern) for each motif, plus the joining colour (D).

Mat motif (make 9 using 3 random colours and black)

Using colour A, make a finger wrap of 3 wraps (see page 44) or ch 5, sl st into a circle.

Round 1: Using A, 12 dc into the circle, sl st to complete round, cut and weave in ends (12 sts).

Round 2: Using B, attach yarn in any st, ch 4 (counts as 1 tr and ch 2 sp), *tr into next st, ch 2, repeat from * to end, sl st to complete round, cut and weave in end (12 spokes).

Round 3: Using C, attach yarn in any ch sp, *ch 5, dc into next sp, repeat from * to end, sl st to complete round, cut and weave in end (12 ch loops).

Round 4: Using D, attach yarn in any loop, ch 6, *dc into next loop, ch 6, repeat from * to end.

Round 5: Continue in D, *7 dc into first loop, repeat from * for each loop, sl st to complete round, cut and weave in ends.

Finishing

Using join as you go (see page 46), join two loops to two loops on each side of adjacent hexagons in the 4th dc of each loop. Join the 9 motifs for a diamond-shaped mat.

Daisy Rug

This diamond-shaped rug is made of nine chunky
daisy motifs, giving maximum impact while being relatively
quick to make. Perfect in a bathroom or a bedroom, it will
bring a dash of springtime optimism to any colour scheme.

Finished size

33½ x 21½in (86 x 54.5cm)

You will need

- Approximately 10½oz (300g) 100% Aran wool in blue (C), plus small quantities of yellow (A) and cream (B). I used Colinette Skye in Adonis Blue (C), Jay (for centre flower), Wasabi Squeeze (A) and Undyed (B)
- 8mm (UK0:USL/11) crochet hook

Tension

Each motif is approximately 7¼in (18.5cm) in diameter.

Daisy motif (make 9)

Using 2 strands of A worked as one, make a 2-finger wrap of 3 wraps (see page 44) or ch 6, sl st into circle.

Round 1: Using A, ch 2 (counts as tr), 11 tr into circle, sl st to complete round, cut and weave in end (12 tr).

Round 2: Using 2 strands of B, attach yarn in any st, ch 1 (counts as dc), dc into same st, *2 dc into next st, repeat from* to end, sl st to complete round, cut and weave in end (24 dc).

Round 3: Using 2 strands of C, attach yarn in any st, ch 2 (counts as tr), tr in next st, ch 6, *tr in next 4 sts, ch 6, repeat from * to end, finishing with a tr in last 2 sts, sl st to complete round (6 loops).

Round 4: Continue using same colour, *11 tr into ch loop, miss 2 sts, sl st into sp before next st, miss 2 sts, repeat from * to end, sl st to complete round, cut off and weave in end (6 petals).

Finishing

Join as you go (see page 46) on the 5th st of 2 petals at a time, or stitch the motifs together using matching yarn, into a diamond pattern of 9 motifs.

Granny's tip

To make a smaller mat, join seven motifs into a hexagon shape.

Giant Cushion

This large cushion is made from four large circles
on each side. The addition of granny triangles turns your
circles into easy-to-join squares. Each side is a different
colour scheme so you can match the look to your mood.

Finished size
Approximately 23in (58.5cm) square

You will need
Random colours side (on page 133)
- 14 x 1¾oz (50g) balls 50% alpaca/
  50% merino yarn or 100% Aran
  wool in 14 different colours.
  I used Rooster Almerino Aran
  in Cornish, Strawberry Cream,
  Custard, Brighton, Ocean,
  Hazelnut, Lolly, Coral, Sorbet,
  Sandcastle, Beach, Smoothie; Ella
  Rae Classic Heathers in Pea Green
  Heather; Ella Rae Superwash
  Classic in Tomato.

Matching squares side (see left)
- 2 x 1¾oz (50g) balls 50% alpaca/
  50% merino yarn for corners (C)
- 2 x 1¾oz (50g) balls 50% alpaca/
  50% merino yarn for joining
  squares (H)
- 6 x 1¾oz (50g) balls 50% alpaca/
  50% merino yarn in different
  colours (A, B, D, E, F, G).
  I used Rooster Almerino Aran in
  Sugared Almond (A), Lolly (B),
  Rooster (C), Coral (D), Beach
  (E), Ocean (F), Brighton (G) and
  Gooseberry (H).
- 4.5mm (UK7:US7) crochet hook
- Stitch marker (optional)
- 5 large buttons, approximately 1in
  (2.5cm) in diameter

Tension
Each square measures approximately
11in (28cm).

Circle (make 8, 4 in each colour scheme)
Using A, make finger wrap of 3 wraps
(see page 44) or ch 5, sl st into a circle.

Round 1: Using A, ch 2 (counts as 1 tr),
11 tr into circle, sl st to complete round,
cut and weave in end (12 tr).

Round 2: Using B, attach yarn to any
st, 2 dc in each st, sl st to complete
round, cut and weave in end (24 sts).

Round 3: Using C, attach yarn to
any st, ch 3 (counts as 1 dtr), 3 dtr
cluster over next 4 sts (see page 42),
ch 7, *4 dtr cluster over next 4 sts
(see page 42), ch 7, repeat from * to
end, sl st to complete round, cut and
weave in end (6 petals).

Round 4: Using A, attach yarn to
any loop, ch 2 (counts as 1 tr), 8 tr
into same ch loop, ch 1, *9 tr in next
loop, ch 1, repeat from * to end, sl st
to complete round, cut and weave in
end (60 sts–54 tr, 6 ch).

Round 5: Using B, attach yarn to any
ch 1 sp, ch 4 (counts as 1 tr and ch
2 sp), miss 1 st, *tr in next st, ch 2,
miss 1 st, repeat from * to end, sl st
to complete round, cut and weave in
end (30 spokes).

Round 6: Using D, attach yarn to
any sp, ch 2 (counts as 1 tr), tr in
same ch sp, ch 1, *2 tr in next ch sp,
ch 1, repeat from * to end, sl st to
complete round, cut and weave in
end (30 double spokes).

Round 7: Using C, attach yarn into
top of a first tr of any pair of tr in

round 6, dc into next st, dc long st (see page 39) into the spoke of round 5, *dc in next 2 sts, dc long st into next spoke of round 5, repeat from * to end, sl st to complete round, cut and weave in end (90 sts).

Round 8: Using A, attach yarn to any st, dc in every st, sl st to complete round, cut and weave in end (90 sts).

Round 9: Using E, attach yarn to any st, dc in every st, sl st to complete round, cut and weave in end (90 sts).

Round 10: Using F, attach yarn to first st that lines up with 2 dc of round 7, and working the third st around the long st of round 7 (they must line up), *dc in next two sts, dtr post st (see page 40) in next st of round 7, repeat from * to end, sl st to complete round, cut and weave in end (90 sts).

Round 11: Using G, attach yarn to any st, dc in every st, sl st to complete round, cut and weave in end (90 sts).

Round 12: Using D, attach yarn to any st, dc in every st, sl st to complete round, cut and weave in end (90 sts).

Round 13: Using C, attach yarn to any st, ch 2 (counts as 1 tr), 2 tr into same st, miss 2 sts, *3 tr into next st, miss 2 sts, repeat from * to end, sl st to complete round, cut and weave in end (30 granny shells).

Round 14: Using H, attach yarn to any st, ch 2 (counts as tr), tr in every st and in the sp between each granny shell, sl st to complete round, cut and weave in end (120 sts).

Granny-shell corner (make 16)

Mark four corners on each circle with a st marker (every 30 sts).

Round 1: Using C, attach yarn 3 sts from marker, ch 1, miss 2 sts, (1 dtr, 2 tr, ch 2, 2 tr, 1 dtr) in next st (marked st), ch 1, miss 2 sts, sl st into next st, ch 3, miss 2 sts, sl st into next st, turn (2 granny shells).

Round 2: Continue using C, 2 tr into the sp between circle and dtr of round 1, ch 1, (3 tr, ch 2, 3 tr) into the next ch 2 sp (point of triangle), ch 1, (2 tr, 1 dtr) into the next ch 1 sp between the last granny shell and the circle, ch 1, miss 2 sts, sl st into next st (7 sts from the marker), ch 3, miss 2 sts, sl st into next st, turn (4 granny shells).

Round 3: Continue using C, 2 tr into first ch 1 sp, ch 1, 3 tr into next ch 1 sp, ch 1, (3 tr, ch 2, 3 tr) into next ch 2 sp (point of triangle), ch 1, 3 tr into next ch 1 sp, ch 1, (2 tr, 1 dtr) into last sp between circle and granny triangle, ch 1, miss 2 sts, sl st into next st (10th st from marker), ch 3, miss 2 sts, sl st into next st, turn (6 granny shells).

Round 4: Continue using C, 2 tr into first ch 1 sp, ch 1, (3 tr into next ch 1 sp, ch 1) twice, (3 tr, ch 2, 3 tr) into next ch 2 sp (point of triangle), ch 1, (3 tr into next ch 1 sp, ch 1) twice, (2 tr, 1 dtr) into last sp between circle and granny triangle, ch 1, miss 2 sts, sl st into next st (13th st from marker), cut off and weave in end (8 granny shells).

Granny-shell joining round

Using H, start in a corner, ch 2 (counts as tr), (2 tr, ch 2, 3 tr) in first corner, ch 1, *(granny shell in next sp, ch 1) 3 times, granny shell in last ch 1 sp between corner triangle and circle, ch 1, miss 1 st, granny shell in next st, ch 1, miss 1 st, granny shell in next st, ch 1, granny shell in next ch 1 sp between circle and corner triangle, ch 1, (granny shell in next sp, ch 1) 3 times, (3 tr, ch 2, 3 tr, ch 1) in corner sp, repeat from * to end, sl st to complete round, cut and weave in end (12 granny shells on each side). Join as you go (see page 46), with sl st in every ch 1 sp between each granny shell for each square until you have 2 blocks of 4 squares making a front and a back, using one of each colour way for a reversible cushion.

Finishing

Join the front and back together matching st for st, working dc in every st, and 2 dc in each corner. Leave one side open and dc around both halves of cushion. Add 4 rows of dc along one half of the opening, as a button band. Add the buttons to the button band, equally spaced. Use the holes of the granny shells as buttonholes.

Abbreviations

ch	chain stitch
ch sp(s)	chain space(s)
cm	centimetre(s)
dc	double crochet
dc2tog	double crochet two stitches together (decrease by one stitch)
dtr	double treble
htr	half treble
in	inch(es)
m	metre(s)
mm	millimetres(s)
sl k	slip knot
sl st	slip stitch
sp	space
st(s)	stitch(es)
tog	together
tr	treble
tr2tog	treble crochet two stitches together (decrease by one stitch)
yd	yard(s)
*	work instructions following * then repeat as directed
( )	repeat instructions inside brackets

Conversions

Crochet hooks

UK	Metric	US
14	2mm	–
13	2.25mm	B/1
12	2.5mm	–
–	2.75mm	C/2
11	3mm	–
10	3.25mm	D/3
9	3.5mm	E/4
–	3.75mm	F/5
8	4mm	G/6
7	4.5mm	7
6	5mm	H/8
5	5.5mm	I/9
4	6mm	J/10
3	6.5mm	K/10.5
2	7mm	–
0	8mm	L/11
00	9mm	M–N/13
000	10mm	N–P/15

UK/US crochet terms

UK	US
Double crochet	Single crochet
Half treble	Half double crochet
Treble	Double crochet
Double treble	Treble crochet

Note: This book uses UK crochet techniques

Suppliers

General supplies

UK

Deramores
Units 5–9 Tomas Seth Business Park
Argent Road
Queenborough
Kent ME11 5TS
Tel: +44 (0)1795 668144
www.deramores.com

Hobbycraft
Parkway
Centrum 100 Business Park, Unit 1
Burton Upon Trent
Staffordshire DE14 2WA
Tel: +44 (0)1202 596100
or 0330 026 1400 (UK only)
www.hobbycraft.co.uk

Laughing Hens
The Croft Stables
Station Lane
Great Barrow
Cheshire CH3 7JN
Tel: +44 (0)1829 740903
www.laughinghens.com

USA

Stitch Diva Studios
848 N. Rainbow Blvd. #688
Las Vegas, NV 89107
www.stitchdiva.com

Yarns and threads

FRANCE

Renaissance Dyeing
Andie Luijk
Place Théophile Delcasse
09600, Montbel d'en Bas
Ariège
Tel: +33 (0)4 6831 5323
www.renaissancedyeing.com

JAPAN

Avril
67-21 Nishinokyo Shokushi-cho
Nakagyo-ku
Kyoto 604-8381
Tel: +81 (0)75 803 1520
www.avril-kyoto.com

UK

Colinette Yarns
Llanfair Caereinion
Powys SY21 0SG
Tel: +44 (0)1938 810128
www.colinette.com

Colour Mart
Unit 2A, Archers Way
Battlefield Enterprise Park
Shrewsbury
Shropshire SY1 3GA
www.colourmart2.com

Loremar
94 High Street
Hythe
Kent CT21 5LE
www.loremar.co.uk

Purplelinda Crafts
39 Firthview Drive
Inverness IV3 8NS
www.purplelindacrafts.co.uk

RKM Wools
4a Roushill
Shrewsbury
Shropshire SY1 1PQ
Tel: +44 (0)1743 245623
www.rkmwools.co.uk

Rooster Yarns
The Croft Stables
Station Lane
Great Barrow
Cheshire CH3 7JN
Tel: +44 (0)1829 740903
www.roosteryarns.com

Stylecraft Yarns
PO Box 62
Goulbourne Street
Keighley
West Yorkshire BD21 1PP
Tel: +44 (0)1535 609798
www.stylecraft-yarns.co.uk

USA
Habu Textiles
99 Madison Avenue
Suite 503
New York, NY 10016
Tel: +1 888 667 4030
www.habutextiles.com

Resources

Books

10-20-30 Minutes to Learn to Crochet
Leisure Arts, 2011

99 Granny Squares to Crochet
Leisure Arts, 2011

100 Flowers to Knit and Crochet by Lesley Stanfield
Search Press Ltd, 2009

100 Snowflakes to Crochet by Caitlin Sainio
Search Press Ltd, 2012

200 Crochet Blocks for Blankets, Throws and Afghans:
Crochet Squares to Mix and Match by Jan Eaton
David & Charles, 2005

300 Classic Blocks for Crochet Projects by Linda P. Schapper
Lark, 2012

Around the Corner Crochet Borders by Edie Eckman
Storey Publishing LLC, 2010

Au Fil des Couleurs: Mon Univers au Crochet
by Cécile Balladino
Le Temps Apprivoisé, 2014

Beyond the Square: Crochet Motifs by Edie Eckman
Storey Publishing LLC, 2008

The Crochet Bible: The Complete Handbook for Creative
Crocheting by Sue Whiting
David & Charles, 2007

Crochet Bohème by Cécile Balladino
Le Temps Apprivoisé, 2013

Crochet Bouquet: Easy Designs for Dozens of Flowers
by Suzann Thompson
Lark, 2008

Crochet Workshop: Learn How to Crochet
with 20 Inspiring Projects by Erika Knight
Quadrille Publishing Ltd, 2012

The Encyclopedia of Crochet Techniques
by Jan Eaton
Search Press Ltd, 2006

Essential Crochet: 30 Irresistible Projects
for You and Your Home by Erika Knight
Quadrille Publishing Ltd, 2006

The Essential Handbook of Crochet Stitches
by Betty Barnden
Search Press Ltd, 2009

The Granny Square Book: Timeless Techniques
and Fresh Ideas for Crocheting Square by Square
by Margaret Hubert
Creative Publishing International, 2011

Granny Squares: 20 Projects with a Vintage Vibe
by Susan Pinner
GMC Publications Ltd, 2014

Websites

etsy.com
This is a great site for sales if anyone wants to try their hand at selling their crochet or just browsing for inspiration.

ravelry.com
A crochet and knitting community with handy advice.

pinterest.com
A wonderful international site full of crochet patterns and inspirational pictures.

youtube.com
Useful for instructional videos of crochet techniques.

Blogs and inspiration

shropshirescrappersuz.blogspot.co.uk
My own blog spot with free patterns and interesting crochet for all levels.

danielacerri.blogspot.co.uk
Italian blog for books and information from Daniela Cerri.

frenchneedle.com/collections/scarves-sophie-digard
Gorgeous colours and ideas to inspire from Sophie Digard.

gipsybazar.blogspot.co.uk
Enjoy a riot of colour on Cécile Balladino's website.

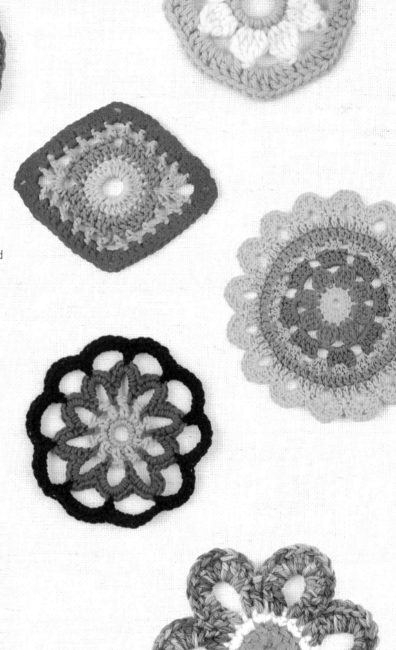

Author's acknowledgements

Another huge thank you to my family. Phil, sorry I got a bit grumpy as deadlines approached. James, thank you for bringing the gorgeous Beth into the family. She has been more help than she will ever know.
Thanks to the GMC team for making this second book possible.

Last, but most importantly, thank you to the wonderful online community of crocheters and to everyone who enjoyed my first book, *Granny Squares*. I thank you for your love and support. I hope you enjoy *Granny Squares and Shapes* too. Thank you all!

Publishers' acknowledgements

GMC would like to thank the following for their help in creating this book: Tess Dimos for modelling, Virginia Armstrong for lending us her lovely house as a photographic location, and Anthony Bailey for still-life shots.

To place an order, or to request a catalogue, contact:

GMC Publications Ltd

Castle Place, 166 High Street, Lewes, East Sussex, BN7 1XU

United Kingdom

Tel: +44 (0)1273 488005

www.gmcbooks.com

Index

abbreviations   137

Beanie Bowl   81–83
Black-edged Lace Mat   124–127
blocking   48
Bright Collar   97–99

Cami Top   85–87
care instructions   48
chain circle   44, 45
chain stitch   38
circles   51
cluster stitch   42
coasters   127
colour   53
Colourful Dish   112–115
conversions   137
Cotton Summer Slippers   56–59
crochet hooks   32, 37, 137

Daisy Rug   128–131
Daisy Top   92–95
Decorative Stool Cover   60–63
decreasing   42, 43
double crochet   39
double crochet long stitch   39
double crochet seams   47
double-sided pieces   36
double treble   40, 41
double treble cluster   42, 43
double treble post stitch   40
doubling yarns   35
dry blocking   48

equipment   32–33

finger wraps   44, 45
Flower-petal Wrap   72–75
Flowery Hairband   64–67
Foot Decoration   105–107

Giant Cushion   132–135

hair ornaments   88
Heart Bunting   109–111
hexagons   51
holding your work   37
hooks   32, 37, 137

increasing   42, 43

joining   46

magic circle   44, 45
mats   63, 115, 124–127
mattress stitch   47
Mini Bag   100–103
mixing yarns   35

over stitch   47

Pillow Cover   68–71
Pinwheel Shawl   120–123
placemats   63
problem solving   49

resources   140–141

seams   47
sewing up   47
shapes   50–51
Shawl Pin   88–91
shell stitch   42, 43
slip knot   37
slip stitch   39
squares   50, 51
suppliers   138–139

techniques   36–49
tension   33, 35
tools   32–33
treble cluster   42, 43
treble crochet   40, 41
Triangle Lap Blanket   117–119
triple treble cluster   42

UK/US conversions and terms   137

Vintage-look Beret   77–79

weaving in ends   44
weight of yarn   34
wet blocking   48
whip stitch   47
working in the round   36, 44, 45

yarns   34–35, 37, 138–139